"In this powerful book, Laura [...] course to peace, rest and the fu[...] life. You will experience freed[...] have a personal encounter with the Prince of Peace. Get ready to turn your stress into rest, your doubt into dreams, and your fear into faith."

Dr. Kynan Bridges, author, pastor, social media influencer;
Kynan Bridges Ministries, Inc.

"In a world filled with confusion, doubt, frustration and fear, Dr. Laura provides us with practical methods to counteract the plans of the enemy. It is a formula that brings health to the body, clarity to the mind and strength to the spirit, which is your God-given right as a child of God."

Dr. Rucele Consigny, professor, Tennessee State University

"Like many of us, Laura Harris Smith has pushed herself through chronic stress, overachievement and nagging nighttime worry. Burning the candle at both ends saps the strength and sharpness of mind needed to fulfill the calling the Lord has on our lives. It has to stop. Take this journey with Dr. Laura and learn to rest peacefully and restoratively again!"

Dr. Jennifer Hayden Epperson, executive director, Kinship Radio
Network, Mankato, MN; author, *The Pioneer's Way*

"*Give It to God and Go to Bed* brought waves of reaffirming and life-changing revelation. This practical teaching imparts renewed knowledge regarding how our spirits control our physical lives. Combining the role and importance of sleep resulted in the dynamic, groundbreaking revelation that is the heart of this dynamic teaching."

Dr. Paul M. Graden, school administrator, Bible professor,
executive pastor, McClain Christian Academy (retired)

"It's rare that a book is filled so beautifully with mind-challenging metaphors, soul-stirring stories and spirit-revealing truths, but this book delivers! If you know people who struggle with sleep deprivation, unforgiveness, spiritual oppression or chronic physical issues, I urge you to get them this book—they will love you for it."

Dr. Bill Greenman, president, Global Purpose Strategies

"Laura Harris Smith absolutely hits the nail on the head to render powerless the killers of anxiety, worry and lack of peace. To overcome each equates to understanding and experiencing the peace of God. Each word of this book is satisfying to the soul. Ten thumbs up!"

Dr. Mark Sherwood, co-CEO, Functional Medical Institute

"The answers to your healing are all here. Stress, the silent killer. Knowing God's will for your life. How to escape the second death. Interpersonal relationships. The problems standing before you. Dr. Laura takes many chronic diseases and the science of stress and provides practical, easy-to-understand remedies from God's Word. He who has ears to hear, let him hear!"

Dr. H. K. Vickery, chairman, Oliver-Mann, Inc.,
A Cancer Solution Mission

GIVE IT TO GOD
AND GO TO BED

GIVE IT TO GOD AND GO TO BED

Stress Less, Sleep Better, Dream More

LAURA HARRIS SMITH, N.D.

Chosen
a division of Baker Publishing Group
Minneapolis, Minnesota

© 2021 by Laura H. Smith

Published by Chosen Books
11400 Hampshire Avenue South
Bloomington, Minnesota 55438
www.chosenbooks.com

Chosen Books is a division of
Baker Publishing Group, Grand Rapids, Michigan

Printed in the United States of America

Library of Congress Cataloging-in-Publication Data

Names: Smith, Laura Harris, author.
Title: Give it to God and go to bed : stress less, sleep better, dream more / Laura Harris Smith.
Description: Minneapolis, Minnesota : Chosen Books, [2021]
Identifiers: LCCN 2021015682 | ISBN 9780800762490 (casebound) | ISBN 9780800799182
   (paperback) | ISBN 9781493433636 (ebook)
Subjects: LCSH: Stress (Psychology)—Religious aspects—Christianity. | Sleep—Religious
   aspects—Christianity. | Insomnia.
Classification: LCC BV4908.5 .S6524 2021 | DDC 248.8/6—dc23
LC record available at https://lccn.loc.gov/2021015682

This publication is intended to provide helpful and informative material on the subjects addressed. Readers should consult their personal health professionals before adopting any of the suggestions in this book or drawing inferences from it. The author and publisher expressly disclaim responsibility for any adverse effects arising from the use or application of the information contained in this book.

Cover design by LOOK Design Studio

21 22 23 24 25 26 27   7 6 5   4 3 2 1

For Campsmith

CONTENTS

Contents

Nightly video blessings for Laura's "10 Days to a Lifetime of Deeper Sleep and Dreams" program can be found at www.LauraHarrisSmith.com/GoodnightVideos

ACKNOWLEDGMENTS

I have people ask me all the time how I accomplish the quantity of work that I do. They either jokingly say that I run circles around them, or they roll their eyes and say they get exhausted just watching me. Well, I have a few secrets, and I humbly but highly recommend them to you: (1) Honor the Sabbath with a *full* day of rest each week (see Exodus 20:8–11), and God will multiply your speed, favor and proficiency during the other six days. (2) Put only good things in your mouth so that God can renew your youth like the eagle's (see Psalm 103:5) and you feel decades younger than you actually are. And (3) Pray for a "double portion," as Elisha did (see 2 Kings 2:9), so that you experience an extra dose of God's Holy Spirit and thus live a life of double blessing and adventure.

But while doing all of those things will get you a life teeming with opportunity and productivity, it also begs for more spiritual warfare in the form of constant resistance. So my final trade secret is this: Choose wisely a prayer team of mature people who have your best interests at heart . . . who will intercede for you daily . . . who will wave torches of fiery prayer and scare away the little foxes and wolves for you . . . whom you can email with an SOS and suddenly have from them an inbox full of prophetic insight and encouragement . . . who will love you in all your forms, keep your most private confidences and *never* judge you. Be willing to let them come and go as they need to, for there are seasons. But just make sure you love and spoil them, for at the end of each project, you will find that they were your secret sauce. And here are the ingredients in mine at the time of the writing, editing and publication of *Give It to God and Go to Bed*:

Elaine Anderson
Trish Beverstein
Jeffrey Lee Brothers
Jennifer Callaway
Debbie Clark
Rusty Consigny
Jeffery and Lisa Dunn
David and Dawn Gray
Jeff and Anady Jensen
Shekinah Svolto Moreira
Mike and Donna Svolto
Sue Teubner
Barry and Fay Wallage

Some of you have been with me for more than a quarter of a century! With others, it feels as though we have been family for even longer. Every prayer you pray is like liquid gold, and I honor you today for every prayer—large and small—that you have sown into me, my family, my business and my ministry. May it all boomerang back to you! I love you so. Now on to the next assignment!

THE DISTRACTION
DOWN THE HALL

How has your day been, so far? On a scale of 1 to 10, with 10 being "very much" and 1 being "not at all," how stressful has it been? Think about your stress level right now. Perhaps you just had a mind-consuming workday, and a looming deadline has you planning an evening of even more work. Perhaps you are outnumbered by children and cannot remember the last time you got a full night's sleep. Maybe you bought this book at an airport kiosk and are finally relaxing after rushing to make your flight. Or maybe you are lonely and are missing the bustle of your once-active life or the company of a lost loved one. Stress takes on many forms and looks different for everyone.

I have prayed for this book to be so saturated in peace that when you pick it up and open its pages, you actually take a deep cleansing breath, feel your shoulders drop, and forget your deadlines and distractions for a while. Reading it may be your one daily act of self-care, and I want you to feel as though you are having a conversation with a good friend who is devoted to seeing you happy and healthy. Imagine having someone just waiting to sit with you and help you manage the day's challenges, who will guide you toward a less stressful and more productive tomorrow. Well, you do have someone like that. While I am not He, I know I am called to help you practice His presence. Since one of the Holy Spirit's names is "Helper," just think of me as the Helper's helper.

Here is my vow to you: I am devoting myself to helping you change the way you process your daytime stresses and nighttime burdens. If you will glance over this book's chapter titles, you will notice that each one contains a preposition: "The Monsters *in* Your Closet." "The Weapons *under* Your Pillow." "The World *outside* Your Window." "The Writing *on* the Wall." The entire book is set in your bedroom, where we are going to tuck you in, get you to sleep, revive your dream life and fill your prayer life with purpose and peace. So whatever your *pre*-position as you begin, prepare yourself for taking a new position altogether.

With each chapter, you are going to find yourself better equipped to pick your battles and not live under the sway of constant confrontation. But because of your new posture, you will also experience what feels like fewer battles since you will be making the daily divine exchange that empties out the battlefields of your life—your worries exchanged for God's weapons. Your worry does not fight off your enemies. But God's weapons do.

My six children were spread out over a period of about sixteen years (they were all about three years apart), so we never had a lot of fighting in our house since each child had his or her own time as "the baby," and then matured into a new phase of childhood by the time the next one came along. Not only that, but practically speaking, a thirteen year old does not fight with a three year old, and a sixteen year old does not fight with a baby. And my two closest in age were numbers three and four—the middle children—and they were so calm and steady that they were not given to fighting (they still are not). So we really did not have much fighting among our kiddos. Granted, foolishness is still bound up in the heart of a child. I was also still outnumbered and definitely had my work cut out for me, but I do not remember ever having to break up a physical fight or a sibling screaming match. The things Chris and I fought in our home were more corporate and internal—our minimal finances, our maturation as very young parents, my unpredictable health—but we fought these things as a team and rarely had to deal with the sideshow of sibling rivalry.

My oldest daughter, on the other hand, also has six children. And she had them in *six years*. When the twin boys were nine months old she got pregnant with the third boy, so she had three in diapers or pull-ups when she got pregnant with the fourth. Then two more singletons and she was done, and now they all are school aged. That means they will all be learning to drive (and all be added to insurance policies) at about the same time, all be in college (or be looking at colleges) at the same time, and all be moving out in what will seem like the blink of an eye. But it also means that right now, they are all sharing the same toys, spaces, friends, and one day soon, girlfriend and boyfriend pools. Jessica's maternal career looks very different from mine, although we have the same number of children.

Is it harder to do all your mothering at once over a shorter number of years, or have it spread out over 36 years, as was the case with my husband and me? (Only in the last year have we become empty nesters, and we already have eleven grandchildren, with grandmuffin number twelve now on the way!) There are challenges in both scenarios, and grace for both. But I remember when Jessica's young teens were tiny, and they would come over to play at "Papa and Lollie's" (our grandmuffins' names for us). Usually, there was a spat to mediate or a toy to get back into the hands of its rightful owner.

These half a dozen siblings did amazingly well, and they will all be great at fractions because they had to share everything and split it six ways. The three boys are so close in age that they basically functioned as triplets, so they were together nonstop, had no memories apart from one another, and were each other's greatest allies. Yet in the blink of an eye, they could pivot and become archenemies! I remember once when they were preschool aged, one boy took a toy from another and ran off with it. Before I could intervene to issue justice, "brudder" had run to retrieve it, but not without a tug-of-war and a shove that left the offender in tears, flat on his back on our concrete floors.

> We need to learn how to pick our battles, letting Papa God fight for us so that we are not stressed-out, worrisome, workaholic insomniacs.

Of course, immediate remorse came and the shover quickly said he was sorry, for he truly was. But afterward, Chris had to sit him down and say this: "If you would have come to Papa when he stole that toy from you, then I could have handled it for you so you didn't have to fight. But now, Papa can't punish him because you've already punished him for me, and trust me, he would have remembered Papa's punishment longer and would never steal anything from you again!"

So it is with you and me, friend. We need to learn how to pick our battles, letting Papa God fight for us so that we are not stressed-out, worrisome, workaholic insomniacs. Who wants to work with that? Who wants to be married to that? Who wants to *be* that? No one! And it certainly is not good PR for God when His earthside representatives behave that way.

The truth is, someone steals something from you every day, and has done so ever since a childhood playmate took your first treasured toy. Some days it is just minutes stolen that you could not afford to lose, or a lost parking spot that cost you extra energy, or a moment of peace that you lost because of someone else's selfishness. But other days, the losses are more substantial. You may discover that something or someone has stolen your idea, your promotion, your reputation, your spouse or your child.

I am not suggesting that you do nothing about these injustices or that you just put on a funny movie to forget that they exist. Stress is real, pain is hard and loss is unjust. But I am suggesting that at some point each day, after the sun goes down, you will have to make the choice to give it all to God and go to bed. The alternative is that your troubles do jumping jacks in front of you and keep you up too late either eating in the kitchen, vegging out on the living-room sofa or slaving away in your home office. Those other rooms and the activities you do in them distract you from making your way down the hall to the bedroom, where you rest and sleep, and where prophetic directional dreams await you.

I see three main thieves that keep you from making that walk to your bedroom each night: stress, work and worry. Let's expose the criminal activities of each of these thieves individually so you can catch them in the act and put a stop to them stealing your sleep, your dreams and your health. We will start with your invisible enemy, stress.

Stress—The Invisible Enemy

Even as you read this, stress may be affecting your physical health without you even knowing it. You may think that your headaches are the result of some undiagnosed ailment, or that your chest pain is surely the sign of a heart attack.[1] You may think that your overeating or undereating is tied to age-related metabolic demands, or that your insomnia is solely due to hormonal changes. It would also be easy to dismiss your lack of productivity at work as being a sign that it is time for a career change, or to figure that your marital dissatisfaction is a sign of the need for a relationship change. In truth, all of these are symptoms of stress. And ignored stress eventually becomes physical *distress*.

There is no end to the unnecessary medical prescriptions written for stress-induced conditions that could all have been averted, had people dealt with the symptoms at their emotional sources. Nothing I ever write is intended to keep you from staying on top of your physical health and visiting your doctor with serious concerns. Quite the opposite. Yet what I am suggesting is that there would be fewer physical concerns in your life if there were less stress.

For example, digestive issues, insomnia, tobacco usage, obesity, diabetes, depression, high blood pressure, social withdrawal, lack of focus, angry outbursts, restlessness, muscle pain, libido changes, fatigue and all the symptoms in the paragraph above are common effects of stress, according to Mayo Clinic,[2] the hospital ranked number one in the nation for the fifth consecutive year.[3] If you are experiencing two or more such symptoms, I urge you not to dismiss them, but to examine your life and look for the stressors. That is why I started out this chapter by asking how stressful your day has been so far, on a scale of 1 to 10. I hope you were able to answer with a low number. If not, then there is the likely possibility that ten years, five years or even one year from now, your physical health will take a drastic turn for the worse if you do not act now.

What is stress? Let's look at the practical definition of both the noun and verb forms, for starters:

Stress *(noun)*
1. strain, pressure, (nervous) tension, worry, anxiety, trouble, difficulty; informal hassle.
2. importance, weight.
3. emphasis, accent, accentuation; beat.
4. pressure, tension, strain.

(verb)
1. emphasize, draw attention to, underline, underscore, point up, place emphasis on, lay stress on, highlight, accentuate, press home.
2. place the emphasis on, emphasize, place the accent on.
3. overstretch, overtax, push to the limit, pressure, make tense, worry, harass.[4]

Whether your stress is a noun or a verb, it has the potential to keep you up at night and prevent you from experiencing the life of peace you were born again to have. The reason for this is found in that second definition of *stress* as a noun: "importance, weight." The things that have the greatest potential to stress you out only have it because they are important to you. I hope it goes without saying that you should not be getting stressed out over the grocery clerk who packs your groceries too slowly or the driver who cuts you off on the interstate. Those people have no real "importance" in your life, and your interactions with them should bear no real "weight" on your day. If you are given to blowing your stack over such insignificant events in your day-to-day life, you are most definitely in danger of developing a stress-induced illness.

It is the things and people who *do* have "importance and weight" with us who have the greatest potential to bring us stress, however, because they also have the greatest potential to bring us joy. That ex-spouse or loved one who hurt you was only able to do so because he or she was important to you. The relationship weighed something on the scales of your life. It is the same with any true friendship you lose. The loss was great because the love was great.

Now look at *stress* as a verb. Do you feel like the third definition—overstretched, overtaxed, pushed to the limit? How about pressured, tense, worried or hassled? If so, it is vital for you to become aware of how to decompress nightly so that your sleep can be sweet, your peace can be full and your health can be protected. By the end of this book, you *will* be able to face your distress and learn how to de-stress. You need God on the scene of your stress, serving as a filter. Before a stressful situation highjacks your day and enters your life, you must consider how you will deal with it and be prepared in advance.

What many do not understand is that stress, anxiety and tension left unchecked can become neurosis. Just listen to this definition of *neurosis* by author Susan M. Turley in *Understanding Pharmacology for Health Professionals*:

The symptoms of neurosis include anxiety, anxiousness, and tension—all at a more intense level than normal—as well as a feeling of apprehension with vague, unsubstantiated fears, but there is never any loss of touch with reality. The treatment of neurosis involves the use of antianxiety drugs, which are also known as anxiolytic drugs or minor tranquilizer drugs. Neurosis is also treated with antidepressant drugs and specific drugs from other categories. Psychiatric drugs are used to treat diseases of the mind, otherwise known as mental illnesses.[5]

But believe it or not, neurosis treatments and antianxiety medications come with a long list of anxiety-causing side effects of their own, and here they are according to the National Institute of Mental Health (NIMH): nausea, blurred vision, headache, confusion, tiredness, nightmares, drowsiness, dizziness, unsteadiness, problems with coordination, difficulty thinking or remembering, increased saliva, muscle or joint pain, frequent urination, and sometimes even rash, hives, swelling of the face or lips, difficulty swallowing, hoarseness, suicidal thoughts and even seizures.[6]

Turley goes on to define *depression*:

> Depression is a mood disorder that is characterized by insomnia, crying, lack of pleasure in any activity, increased or decreased appetite, inability to act or concentrate, with feelings of guilt, helplessness, hopelessness, worthlessness, and thoughts of suicide and death. These symptoms occur daily, interfere with life activities, and last longer than two weeks. The treatment for depression involves the use of antidepressant drugs.[7]

Turley's descriptions are correct, and she is also correct when she describes that the typical treatment for depression involves the use of antidepressant drugs. But the side effects can be devastating. Once again, they are listed on the NIMH website in keeping with those released by the FDA: nausea and vomiting, diarrhea, sleepiness, thoughts about suicide or dying, attempts to commit suicide, new or worsening depression, new or worsening anxiety, feeling very agitated or restless, panic attacks, trouble sleeping (insomnia), new or worsening irritability, acting aggressively, being angry or violent, acting on dangerous impulses, an extreme increase in activity and talking (mania) and other unusual changes in behavior or mood.[8]

Now you know how stress can affect you physically and emotionally. But I will tell you that, as pastors, my husband and I have also seen stress gravely affect people's spiritual health. One day they are stressed about their work—whether it be a demanding boss, a lack of promotion, budgetary cutbacks or a contentious co-worker—and if their stress is left undealt with, they are suddenly taking out their frustrations on handy congregants, and even on their pastors.

I remember one time we had a congregant whose once-enjoyable job became so stressful that he seemed to go through a personality change. Once full of winning smiles, he was now always talking about how bad things were at work. He never talked about a solution, or about finding another job. He just grew increasingly more frustrated and increasingly more unreliable. He began stepping down from his duties at church in order to manage his occupational stress. When some church leaders spoke into his life out of concern, he brought up that he felt he might need to change churches. The situation had a happy ending, but only because he finally dealt with the source of his stress instead of rearranging his life to accommodate it. He had to learn his own worth so that he could set a course for his future and not let himself be taken advantage of.

Likewise, it is in your best interest—body, mind and spirit—not to let your stressors go unchecked. Face them head-on. We will deal more with how to do that in chapter 9, but next let's take a look at a second thief that will try to entice you away from peaceful sleep—work.

Work—The Enticing Seducer

Another distraction that keeps you from heading to bed each night is work. Oh, how I love work! In my idea of a perfect world, I would never have to sleep and could just work all day and night. I would never grow tired, get mentally dim and have to turn in for the night. To be honest, it is the greatest temptation of my life— the seduction of sleeplessness. I battle it the way some people battle addiction or the lust of the flesh. I literally get a second wind about midnight each night, and since the world has finally gone to sleep and is no longer texting or calling me, I feel as if a window of productivity opens up and I am able to climb through it, sprout wings and fly.

My secret wish is that there is no sleep in heaven. Rest, but no sleep! I get so much accomplished after midnight that I feel as if I have cheated tomorrow out of a few good working hours that no one else in the world is getting. Granted, I almost killed myself doing that for several decades. Then in 2012, it all came crashing down when my sleep defiance caught up with me and I wound up in adrenal burnout. This condition is a severe adrenal insufficiency caused by stress, sleeplessness and other factors. When you do not or cannot sleep to replenish yourself each night, your body must manufacture its energy from other sources in order for all your body systems to keep operating and for you to feel like getting out of bed in the morning. Most often, your body places the demand on your adrenaline and cortisol hormones to accomplish both. The trouble is, once you run out of adrenaline and cortisol, your days are numbered.

Also called adrenal fatigue or adrenal exhaustion, the worst manifestation of this condition is in stage 4, when your internal organs and body systems shut down entirely. By the time I was diagnosed I was already in stage 3, and basically I was told to "make changes or die." My nutritionist told me that if I survived at all, it would take me 18 to 24 months to turn myself around. Another name for this condition is Addison's disease, a disorder many people first heard about after the death of John F. Kennedy. It was said that he had it so badly that had he not been assassinated, he would have been dead anyway within a year.

Although some of its names suggest fatigue or exhaustion, I never experienced those as severely as some people with the condition, who say they cannot even get out of bed. Because of my strong constitution, I never really felt so drained that I could not function. And due to the work ethic I inherited from my parents, I just kept pushing myself day by day through my busy life. Most of my days were twenty-hour days, or close to it. Yet I definitely noticed a difference when I asked my body to climb a flight of stairs, or when I tried to stay on my feet all day.

While in my early forties, at five foot two and under 110 pounds, I went in for an annual doctor's checkup and showed a dramatic increase in my cholesterol and blood sugar levels. On the decrease was my adrenal function as my reproductive system came to a screeching halt—all confirmed by blood, urine and saliva tests. My body temperature got down to as low as 94.5 (one morning it got as low as 89.9, confirmed by a second thermometer), which revealed an apathetic thyroid. This meant a sluggish metabolism that eventually came to a stop and resulted in unwanted weight gain.

Not only had my adrenals quit producing sufficient adrenaline (necessary for energy), but they had also all but quit producing cortisol (necessary for reducing stress). Even my digestive track was showing the presence of bad bacteria in my small intestines, which is dangerous for many reasons, including that it leaves your immunities compromised since more than 70 percent of your immune system is in your gut. My pancreas was in total rebellion, and blood tests showed I was pre-diabetic. This was after an entire lifetime of perfectly healthy blood sugar that, if anything, always registered a bit on the low side.

My neurological health took a hit, too, in the form of a sudden increase in the small seizures that I had been experiencing for almost forty years by this point. Since sleep deprivation is the number-one seizure trigger, my lack of good sleep health led to poor neurological health. All of this and so much more was highjacking my life, including a mysterious brain fog that I simply could not shake, even on the days when I felt my strongest and most like myself. My creative juices also seemed nonexistent, and I experienced writer's block for the first time in my life.

Still, I was not making the connection between my excessive work, my lack of sleep and my failing body. Then I began doing research for a book I was writing called *Seeing the Voice of God: What God Is Telling You through Dreams and Visions* (Chosen, 2014). I had felt led to introduce a new spin on dreams books by including in mine medical studies on the body's sleep stages, along with other nutritional nuggets such as how to increase dream recall through the use of certain vitamins and minerals. I knew I had to start by interviewing a sleep study doctor, and after contacting the offices of numerous pulmonologists in Nashville with my request, one nibbled. You can read those studies for yourself in *Seeing the Voice of God*, but suffice it to say that as I sat in Starbucks the day of our interview, feverishly taking notes, I had no idea that God was setting me up to discover what was wrong with me. He was using work to make me study sleep, because it was work that was keeping me from sleeping.

As the doctor I interviewed explained that day, the first consequence of sleep deprivation is hormonal failure. You would think that when I heard that fact, I would have had a lightbulb moment. But I did not. Keep in mind that this was before I was diagnosed with adrenal burnout. Still, the symptoms were there that every hormone in my body was decreasing. Now, as a naturopath, I know that since hormones are synthesized largely from cholesterol (along with every cell in your body), that was why my high cholesterol levels had climbed higher. My body was fighting itself to produce hormones, but it was a losing battle for both sides. I was never going to regain sufficient production of my thyroid, adrenal or reproductive hormones if I did not make changes.

> If there is one thing I have learned from this experience, it is that if you do not go to bed and sleep, your organs will go to sleep for you.

I had a thirty-year sleep debt to pay, and the bill was coming due. If there is one thing I have learned from this experience, it is that if you do not go to bed and sleep, your organs will go to sleep for you. I had thought that because I ate my veggies, exercised regularly and avoided bad fats and sugary foods, I was in good health. But even if you do all of that, sleep deprivation can still take you to an early grave if you do not set new habits. It was time for me to do just that.

Since my liver also showed signs of struggling, I could not just start popping pills tailor-made for each organ, because then my liver could not process them all. I had to use food as medicine and get a crash course in herbology, vitamins, minerals and more. With the steps I took and the changes I made, what should have taken up to two years to turn around took my Great Physician and me only six months to accomplish.

You can read the full story of how I survived in my book *The 30-Day Faith Detox: Renew Your Mind, Cleanse Your Body, Heal Your Spirit* (Chosen, 2016). That was the book I wrote that came from the whole adrenal burnout and recovery experience. It still blows my mind that now, tens of thousands of people from all over the world have followed the same month-long, total-temple cleanse I presented in that book and have found healing—physically, emotionally and spiritually. You may want to follow the regimen I outlined there yourself. It truly is a reset button for the body, mind and spirit, and not a day goes by that I do not hear from people who are beginning or ending their faith detox journey. They express their excitement, list their accomplishments and testify about the medications they have come off of and the healing they have found in their relationships. God is so good! But also remember that the key to good physical health is no longer just diet and exercise. It is now diet, exercise *and sleep*. And as I now believe and will never tire of saying, *sleep doctors could put all the other doctors out of business, because once you fix your sleep, you fix your whole health!*

Before it is too late, you must learn to take the stressors we have discussed and give them to God, shut your laptop and stop working, and then will yourself to go to bed. We will discuss more in chapter 2 about how to improve your sleep health and get your sleep debt paid. But first, let's look at the third thief that steals our sleep—worry. This final one excels at causing distractions that often keep us from going to bed, or that keep us wide awake once we get there.

Worry—The Sleep Stealer

Have you ever heard of kudzu? It is an aggressive vine known to almost everyone in the United States, although its origin is from the other side of the world (Japan and southeast China). In my part of the country, we refer to it as "the vine that ate the South." You can see it growing on the roadside along most interstate systems, and it is a perfect example of a plant that was introduced with the best of intentions but with the worst of outcomes.

Kudzu first came to America in 1876 as a display at the Japanese Exhibition of the Philadelphia Centennial Exposition. Immediately after the gathering, all plants in the exhibit were ordered destroyed. By the turn of the century, however, you could buy kudzu in mail-order catalogs, as many people did in an attempt to bring shade to their garden arbors and homes. In the 1930s, kudzu was introduced to America intentionally by the Soil Erosion Service (SES) and the Civilian Conservation Corps (CCC) for the purpose of combatting soil erosion in the Southeast. I only know this history because I used to have a friend whose father was responsible for helping make the decision to bring kudzu to America—a decision that many in the CCC (a work relief program employing millions of people on environmental projects during the Great Depression) would go on to regret.

True, kudzu vines provide protection of a sort for wide-open landmasses by preventing soil erosion, but the problem with this climbing perennial is that it can overtake entire fields of vegetation—grass, trees, flowers and more—in no time at all. In fact, it grows up to a foot a day in the early summer, so that old adage about how you can "watch kudzu grow" is actually accurate. And it basically strangles whatever it touches by slowly wrapping itself around its host. Not only that, but its tuberous roots can reach a depth of twelve feet in older patches and can weigh as much as two hundred to three hundred pounds.

This marvel plant, which was once intended to provide shade and relief, actually kills. Inch by inch and foot by foot, the landscape it invades becomes a thing of the past. Just google the words "kudzu overtaking vegetation" and check out some of the alarming images, including those of how it soon "eats" non-cropland areas such as old buildings, vacant lots and abandoned structures.

Friend, worry is like kudzu. It feels so constructive at first, as if it will produce some sort of solution to whatever problem is nagging you as you are trying to get to sleep each night. Truth be told, worry actually can make you stay up troubleshooting and problem solving until the wee hours, and then you never get to bed at all. But the troubles never get solved as worry wraps itself around your mind and steals your sleep. And for all you daytime worriers, worry can entangle your every waking thought and cause you to make decisions entirely out of fear and not faith.

Just like what kudzu does to whatever it touches, if left unchecked, worry will creep and crawl its way into your decision-making and even your dreaming, if you let it run amuck. Listen to Jesus' words to you about your worry:

> Therefore I say to you, do not worry about your life, what you will eat or what you will drink; nor about your body, what you will put on. Is not life more than food and the body more than clothing? Look at the birds of the air, for they neither sow nor reap nor gather into barns; yet your heavenly Father feeds them. Are you not of more value than they? Which of you by worrying can add one cubit to his stature?
>
> So why do you worry about clothing? Consider the lilies of the field, how they grow: they neither toil nor spin; and yet I say to you that even Solomon in all his glory was not arrayed like one of these. Now if God so clothes the grass of the field, which today is, and tomorrow is thrown into the oven, will He not much more clothe you, O you of little faith?

Therefore do not worry, saying, "What shall we eat?" or "What shall we drink?" or "What shall we wear?" For after all these things the Gentiles seek. For your heavenly Father knows that you need all these things. But seek first the kingdom of God and His righteousness, and all these things shall be added to you. Therefore do not worry about tomorrow, for tomorrow will worry about its own things. Sufficient for the day is its own trouble.

Matthew 6:25–34 NKJV

I have a good friend in Nashville named Trish Beverstein who has a perennial lily field just outside her house. She planted it years ago, and soon after, she began to view it as a reminder and a refuge based on this Matthew 6 passage. When the trials of life come, instead of toiling, spinning or worrying, she just goes and sits in her lily field. It reminds her to seek first the Kingdom of God and then expect excitedly for God to provide her the answers she needs. I have had a front-row seat to Trish's life for decades, and like clockwork, that is what God does for her every time.

Trish and I share a love for many things—nutrition, health and beauty products—but there is no cosmetic like happiness. I am certain that Trish's beauty can be directly attributed to the peace and joy she gets while sitting in her lily field "considering the lilies." Maybe you should plant a lily field, too. Or at least get yourself a lily flower pillow for your bed as a reminder. Then each night, let it woo you to your bedroom, and as you take it off your bed and let it drop to the floor, let go of your worries with it. Refuse to toil and spin. Choose rest.

As we end this first chapter, I want you to answer the questions below, which will help you itemize the three categories of distractions we have talked about that keep you from getting to bed each night and resting peacefully. Write down your stressors, your work deadlines and your worries, which you will refer to later, when you finish the book. As you read each of this book's ten chapters at your own pace, do the same thing. *You are not done with each chapter until you complete its vital accompanying questions.*

Once you are done reading this entire book, you can then start my "10 Days to a Lifetime of Deeper Sleep and Dreams" program, which I introduce in chapter 10. Not only will you use the information you have learned from each chapter along the way, but you will also use your answers to the questions for each of the 10 chapters. Obviously, the program will take you 10 days after you finish reading the book. As you go through it, I encourage you to review each chapter's questions and answers, one night at a time, just before bed. After your review, go to the online link I will provide in the 10-Day program. That link will take you to a special video you can view where I will pray a prayer over you about that day's topics.

But first, here are today's questions and closing prayer:

QUESTIONS AND PRAYER

1. List three stresses or worries that you face on a regular basis right now.

2. Describe your relationship with your work at present.

Pray this out loud: *Father God, please show me the daily distractions that are joining forces to prevent me from ending each day in peace. Highlight for me those places where I choose to toil and troubleshoot instead of trusting You and heading down the hall to my bedroom each night for sweet rejuvenation. Help me to have healthy boundaries for my work and to never allow it to steal my focus from You. In the name of Jesus, Amen.*

THE TREASURES INSIDE YOUR BEDROOM

Do me a favor. Go to your bedroom right now. If you are away from home, close your eyes and walk there in your mind. As you step inside, I want you to sit or lie down upon your bed. *This* is the room in which you should be spending at least one-third of your day. Time spent sleeping in the bedrooms and beds of your past should have composed one-third of your life. If you are 30, you should have slept for 10 years. If you are 45, then for 15 years. And when you are 75, you will have—should have—slept for 25 years of your life. (If you are older than that and are in good health, then I am positive you have good sleep habits!)

It is in this room that many beautiful things should and will take place for you as you rest. Our goal is to discuss them in detail in this chapter, because an important piece of my overall goal is to put tools in your hands to help you give your worries, stress and problems to God each day and get a good night's sleep as He works on them for you. That beautiful exchange happens in the bedroom. But sometimes we treat our bedrooms like a meaningless pit stop where we just plunk down and lie unconsciously for a few hours at the end of a hard day.

Look around you. Whether your bedroom is large or small, it should be comprised of the items that bring a smile to your face and peace to your heart. It should not be where the bills and dirty laundry accumulate. You should walk in and immediately want to smile, take a deep breath and relax. It should be a place of inspiration, a sanctuary where the cares of your day melt away. True, the cares will still be there when you awaken and may not have changed. But you will have changed. You will be stronger and more focused. You should awaken with new purpose and strength each morning.

It is the same thing even if your "bedroom" is a Murphy bed that folds up into the wall, a sleeping bag on a friend's living-room floor or a cot in a shelter. Each night, wherever you lay your body—God's mysteriously miraculous creation intended to be the temple of His Holy Spirit—that place becomes the sacred patch of space where you recline to be restored by the Creator Himself. Can you view it as sacred? Let's look at three main treasures awaiting you in your bedroom: peace, which is the environment for rest; sleep, which is your nightly trip to healing; and dreams, which make your resting place your conference room with God.

Peace—The Environment for Rest

You know that feeling when you walk into a new, clean hotel room and you flip on the lights and first see that big, fluffy bed? You have been traveling, walking, lugging your suitcase or briefcase (or both), and you had to check in and climb the stairs or find the elevator. Then you had to get your keyless entry card to work, and as soon as you see that tiny green light, you enter and are now "home."

I don't know about you, but my frequent practice is to drop everything, slip out of my shoes, step over to the bed and take a front-facing nose dive (or a backward free fall). It is my instinctual reaction. Why do we do that? Because that room represents one thing: rest. Rejuvenation. And at the end of that day, with your busy out-of-town meetings (or for me, often a studio taping), you can hardly wait to get back to it and chillax. Much thought has gone into making that reentry process just as special for you each night you are there, including maid service and a turndown.

> The point is to invest in this one-third of your life by creating an environment of peace in your home—namely, in your bedroom.

But just as traveling too much can diminish this experience night after night, year after year, so it is with our own bedroom at home. We become so familiar with it, and the new wears off. We come home to a bedroom that is messy, smells like dirty socks or kitty litter, and has not been dusted or vacuumed in a month or more. Besides, the lightbulbs in the fixtures are so bright that if you were sleepy before you came home at the end of a long day, forget it now. You are suddenly wide awake.

What if you took five minutes each morning and made your bed, gathered up the junk and started a ten-hour diffuser to greet you with your favorite scent upon your arrival home? And what if you took a little time each weekend to dust and vacuum or sweep, rearrange accessories to keep the bedroom feeling "new," and organize your piles of stuff so that everything has a place and finds its way back there quickly each workday?

The point is to invest in this one-third of your life by creating an environment of peace in your home—namely, in your bedroom. Because chances are that you will not find a place of peace in the kitchen, the garage, the laundry room or any room, other than your own resting space. You don't usually say good-night to your housemates as you walk into the dining room or bathroom. You say it while headed toward your bedroom. Why not make it a place where the Prince of Peace Himself could feel at home? Because if your bedroom is not that kind of place, then it is very unlikely that His peace will be there.

Listen to 2 Thessalonians 3:16: "Now may the Lord of peace himself give you peace at all times in every way. The Lord be with you all." That Greek word for peace, *eirēnē*, means the following:

- security, safety, prosperity, felicity (because peace and harmony make and keep things safe and prosperous)
- exemption from the rage and havoc of war
- peace between individuals, i.e., harmony, concord
- the way that leads to peace (salvation)
- of Christianity, the tranquil state of a soul assured of its salvation through Christ, and so fearing nothing from God and content with its earthly lot, of whatsoever sort that is
- a state of national tranquility
- of the Messiah's peace[1]

With *eirēnē* used twice, this verse could therefore be translated, "May the God of security, safety, prosperity and felicity Himself give you harmony between individuals, a tranquil state where you fear nothing and are content, and an exemption from the rage and havoc of war." Imagine that type of peace—"a state of national tranquility"—in your bedroom! Especially if you are married and there has been fighting between nations that evening. It is the "Messiah's peace," and if you know Him and are in daily relationship with Him, then He is going to follow you to bed each night and tuck you in. And as our verse ends, He will also "be with you," so guess what—He will also be watching over you while you sleep.

Years ago, I was a television shopping channel host on the Shop at Home Network, first as an on-air guest host and eventually getting hired as a full-time TV host in 2006. I sold jewelry, electronics, kitchenware, everyday household items and more. But my all-time favorite shows were the bedding shows. Our trusty production assistants would enter an entirely blank studio space, and within an hour they would create and furnish an entire bedroom on the set, complete with a king or queen bed, dresser, nightstands, wardrobe and even throw rugs, lamps and plants. I have a distinct memory of walking on set one day and seeing them tediously removing every wrinkle out of the drapes with steamers (and we were not selling the drapes or the steamers). They were re-creating an environment. An environment that hopefully you would take one look at, and with watering mouth pick up the phone to place an order.

But you were not buying the furniture or accessories or even the bedframe. The production assistants were going to all that trouble just so I could sell you a plain mattress. Or the sheets. They wanted you to picture yourself in the midst of this paradise, and after they had every spot and wrinkle out of the bedspread and matching bedding, it was then my job to jump up on the bed and sell, sell, sell what was *under* me. Their job was to design a beautiful, peaceful environment so that I could do my job, which was to sell a boring, square, white blob of coils and springs.

The show always started the same way, with a jib camera over me (that long, dinosaur-looking camera that gives shows their large sweeping or "swoop in" moments), as if it were a celestial view, with me looking up into it from this peaceful environment. The camera would pan over and then down onto me there on the bed, and within moments you didn't even know I was trying to sell you a mattress. What I was doing was selling you the concept of peace and rest (so that I could then sell you a mattress). Occasionally, if the mattress was one of those with "NASA technology that withstands even the strongest of g-forces," the producers would have me place a glass of water on one corner at the end of the bed and then go jump up and down on the other end to show that the water did not move at all in the glass. This would prove that not even anyone getting in and out of the bed next to you would interrupt this nocturnal bliss I was selling you. You needed peaceful sleep, and here was your chance. "Don't miss this opportunity!"

And really, that is what I am trying to sell you right here, right now. I am trying to convince you to create an environment in your bedroom that breeds peace. So look around you. Does your bedroom whisper *Peace* . . . ? Or does it scream *Please! Change me* . . . ?

Perhaps you say, "I'd love to create a more peaceful bedroom environment, but I don't have the money for it." Trust me, I have been there. I remember when I was pregnant with my sixth child, Jenesis. Our three bedrooms upstairs were full with five children, and there was no place for a nursery. One night I shot up in bed, crying, and said to my husband, "Where on earth are we going to put her? There's no place for another baby in this house! What are we going to do?!"

Chris, in his usual calm manner, said, "Laura, you're going to put her in a bassinette beside our bed, as you did with all the other newborns. Why on earth would she want to be upstairs with five noisy kids? She doesn't need her own bedroom just yet. Come here; it will be okay."

I lay back down and dried my tears, but still, in my heart I wanted a welcoming place for my baby. I prayed and asked God for a plan. I needed to nest, and when I looked around our dreary bedroom, I felt it was in serious need of a makeover. But there was little to no money in the budget for that. The room contained all brown wicker, a dark bedspread and dark knickknacks scattered here and there. I got creative. I painted the walls lavender, spray-painted all the wicker white (outdoors!), and bought a beautiful yellow-and-white comforter from Kmart. I cleared out the dark knickknacks and replaced them with pastel décor that I gathered here and there from other rooms in the house.

Before long, Jenesis had a beautiful, calming nursery. Her bassinette was white wicker, too, with a beautiful white coverlet. Of course, Chris and I now were sleeping in a nursery, but there was nothing "baby" about it. Just calming and peaceful décor, and I think I spent maybe $50. To this day, it is the room makeover I am most proud of. Although it was twenty years ago and we have done a couple of bedroom makeovers since then that are more "grown-up," that white-and-yellow Kmart comforter is still the one the "kids" fight over when they visit us for a movie night. There is peace baked in. There is faith and creativity baked in.

Necessity is *not* the mother of invention. Father God is the author of all innovation, especially innovation birthed out of desperation. So take some time today to consider a bedroom makeover. Pray the way I did and ask God for a plan to transform your bedroom into a calming atmosphere of peace. Here are ten easy things you can do for free or next to nothing:

1. Reposition your bed to another wall.
2. Clear your room and organize all clutter.
3. Rearrange the pictures or art on your walls.
4. Get rid of any furniture you don't need.
5. Hide all electronic cords.
6. Change the lighting in your room (string lights are inexpensive and calming).
7. Hang your current curtains higher to "increase" the size of the room.
8. Donate any items you don't need (including clothing that is lying around).
9. Add new throw pillows on your bed (or re-cover old ones).
10. Put your bed on inexpensive plastic risers to create storage space underneath.

You can find countless bedroom makeover ideas online, but one article I really liked was *Good Housekeeping* magazine's "45 Inspiring Ways to Create the Bedroom of Your Dreams" (which you can find at www.goodhousekeeping.com/home/decorating -ideas/g1727/bedroom-makeover-ideas/).

Sleep—Your Nightly Trip to Healing

The second treasure you will discover in your bedroom is sleep itself. What happens when you sleep? More than you think! In *Seeing the Voice of God*, I outlined in scientific detail the stages your body goes through as you sleep at night, and we learned that it is really quite a ride. I won't go into that much detail here, but let's at least look at the basics of the sleep stages you enter and exit throughout the night:

Stage 1 (N1): This is a relaxed state of early sleep that you fade into and out of after you climb into bed. You are easily awakened from it and won't even know you were sleeping (and will argue that you were not with those watching), but your brain waves paint a different picture. This is the stage when your muscle activity slows, and you might experience muscle jerks and twitches. Your brain waves are characterized by theta waves, which are slower and wider than your daytime alpha and beta waves. Think of stage 1 as first gear as you shift into sleep. This stage lasts between five and ten minutes.

Stage 2 (N2): Your eyes and body stop moving in this stage; your heart rate and temperature also decrease. *Sleep spindles*, 1-second to 2-second bursts of electrical activity, are added to the theta waves. So are *K complexes*, sizable peak and valley brain waves. Scientists say these types of brain waves help us turn off the outside world. Your body spends 15–20 minutes in this second gear, and then you enter what is officially called "deep sleep."

Stage 3 (N3): The theta waves become delta waves, the slowest and strongest waves our brains produce. You have now left behind the world around you, as well as your stressors and worries. Stage 3 contains only 20 percent to 50 percent of deep sleep delta waves, whereas stage 4 will be marked by a majority of delta activity. Sleepwalking (somnambulism) occurs in this stage. We enter this "third gear" 35–40 minutes after falling asleep.

Stage 4 (still considered N3): In this stage of slow delta wave deep sleep, you are oblivious to external stimuli. This is the slice of night when restorative sleep occurs. The pineal gland releases growth hormone (GH), which results in bone and muscle growth in children, but in adults provides tissue repair and total body rejuvenation. Stop and think of that miracle: The same hormone that makes you grow as a sleeping child makes you heal as a sleeping adult! Because the body also decreases its breakdown of proteins that repair damage from the day's stress and ultraviolet rays, deep sleep becomes your "beauty sleep." Prolactin and gonadotropin are also secreted, which makes this stage a phase of healing and rehabilitation. If something awakens you during this fourth gear of (deep N3) sleep, you will be extremely disoriented.

Before you shift from stage 4 into "fifth gear," which is REM dream sleep, you actually reverse and downshift gears, going from stage 4 back to stage 3 and then landing at stage 2—yet you don't awaken. Then, as if you are pushing up a hill in second gear, you reach the top and begin to coast downward—fast. You skip all the other gears and shift immediately into a proverbial fifth gear. Unlike in stage 2, where your eyes remain still, they now begin moving back and forth quickly as you enter what is called REM (rapid eye movement) sleep. Ah, dreamland!

So your first complete sleep cycle looks like this: stage 1 to 2 to 3 to 4, then back to 3, then 2 . . . then finally into the final phase, REM dream sleep. This kind of sleep cycle repeats four or five times before sunrise, depending on how long you are in bed. Each cycle lasts 90–120 minutes. After the first cycle, you shift gears in a little different order each time. You spend less time per cycle in N3, and more time in N2 and REM sleep. Whereas in the first sleep cycle you spend about 10 minutes in REM dream sleep, the latter sleep cycles have you in almost solid REM dream sleep. With every eight full hours of sleep, you therefore experience between an hour and a half and two hours of dreaming. It is like watching a full-length movie each night in your sleep—for free![2]

But you are doing much more than dreaming as you sleep each night. You are healing. That is the miracle of stage 4, as we just saw, since it is here that tissue repair and total body rejuvenation happens each night. This is also the time of night that your emotional stressors get physically processed. As we established, without this crucial deep sleep stage, you will awaken looking as if you have not gotten your beauty rest. I guess you could say that the fountain of youth is actually underneath your pillow. Best to drink deeply each night!

What if you are among the many who claim they cannot sleep? This is the opposite of the issue I had, which is that I refused to sleep. Instead, you legitimately *cannot* sleep. You develop what I call a sleep debt, and the evidence begins to show up in your day-to-day behavior that involves apparent sleep deprivation. Here are a dozen signs that you may have a significant sleep debt:

1. daytime drowsiness
2. reduced immunity (you get sick often)
3. irritability and mood swings
4. weight gain
5. low libido
6. frequent yawning
7. difficulty concentrating
8. brain fog
9. memory loss and forgetfulness
10. anxiety
11. depression
12. paranoia

In many ways, writing this book takes me back in time to writing my book *Seeing the Voice of God*. I remember so vividly that as I was studying for and researching that book, God put a strong desire in my heart to include medical chapters that would explain the stages of sleep, as well as nutritional advice for how to get a better night's sleep and even for improving dream recall. I have taught on dreams and visions for years, but when it came time to write that book, I told the Lord there were too many other good dream books out there—many written by my heroes of the faith—and that I was not interested in repeating their works. That was when I told the Lord that I would write the book if He could give me a "new spin" on this topic.

Immediately, He drew my attention to the fact that I had never before seen a religious book on dreams and visions that included medical chapters. That thought totally excited and totally petrified me at the same time. I was entirely unqualified to write on anything having to do with the human body, not to mention the physiological reasons behind why or how we sleep. I was not a nutritionist at the time, nor a naturopathic doctor, nor had I studied health in any significant way except perhaps to increase my personal health. As I set out to create that unique book on dreams, I kept hearing the phrase *sleep is the mattress of dreams*. It wound up becoming part of our advertising for the book, but it started as a small phrase that God kept whispering to me over and over again, and I have never forgotten it. You cannot dream if you cannot sleep.

> Sleep is the mattress of dreams.

Suddenly, this phrase created in me an urgent desire to help people sleep better. Keep in mind that I myself was not practicing good sleep health at the time. So in part, God was having me learn all of this to save my life. But I am also convinced, because of the fruit I have seen since that book's publication, that it was indeed a God-inspired word for a sleepless generation.

Something else happened as I was writing that book. I took a freak fall into a glass and wrought-iron coffee table, breaking my rib and puncturing my lung, which resulted in a pneumothorax (collapsing lung). As if I had not been intimidated enough already about gathering all the medical data necessary, now I was having to do so in intense pain worse than any pain I had experienced giving birth to my six children. I refused to take painkillers, however, because I did not want to look back on the book text one day and find it muddy. I needed my thoughts and words to be crystal clear so that I could communicate to my readers why they sleep, how they sleep, where they should sleep, when they should sleep and what the endless benefits are to their health and dream retention, if they would make the necessary changes to improve their sleep health.

Shortly after my fall against the table, I cried out to God and He dramatically healed me of its aftereffects. He instantly patched up my rib and reinflated my lung, and an X-ray confirmed that it was a miracle! I know from experience that God helps me write my books so that I can help you. Here, I want to build upon the important foundation I laid in that book. In these pages, I want to provide you with some updated research and further solutions for your sleep crisis. (But go back and read that other book anyway, since I went through so much pain to write it for you!)

According to the Cleveland Clinic, more than 70 million Americans suffer from sleep disorders[3] and tens of millions more encounter them on and off during their lifetimes. With more than eighty sleep disorders now identified, it is predicted that the sleep medicine industry will hit the $102 billion mark by 2023.[4] In 2017 alone, sleep aids generated almost $70 billion worldwide, and if you even have a simple sleep eye mask in your home, you contributed to this total. Other items in this market are mattresses, pillows, sleep laboratory medications and sleep apnea devices. Treatments for insomnia, sleep apnea, restless leg syndrome, narcolepsy and sleepwalking also fall into this category, along with countless other items that help people get a better night's sleep.

Chances are that you have even bought a few sleep aids yourself, since more than 50 percent of adults say they have experienced bouts of insomnia at some point in their lives. If you have sleep apnea or suspect it, please get tested. I have friends whose lives were changed by an apnea machine, and they make those devices today with masks that hardly touch your face at all.

Sleep deprivation will send you to an early grave, because it is only during deep sleep each night that your body heals and recovers. You may learn to cope emotionally with your sleep debt and function by pushing through each day's exhaustion, but you can never cope with it physically for too long. I know that from experience! You owe it to yourself and your health to pay your sleep debt and set new habits for this invaluable one-third of your life.

I am passionate enough about helping people resolve their sleep issues that I actually created an essential oil blend to help them quiet their brains each night. In fact, the blend is called Quiet Brain® and I will talk a little more about it in another chapter, but it is very effective. Lab tests have proved it crosses the blood-brain barrier to calm the mind. Not only that, but we were also able to get the recipe patented when only 5 percent of natural products ever get a patent from the United States Patent and Trademark Office (USPTO).[5] I will tell you more about that story, too, in a few moments.

God does not want you to suffer any longer from sleep deprivation and sleep debt, and this book is devoted to helping you unravel how you can sleep better, longer and sweeter. Sleep is a sacred time because, remember, it is during this time that you can turn off your mind and allow God to speak to your spirit through prophetic dreams. Consider today that your sleep debt is not just a physical snare that leads to chronic illness, and/or that your sleep defiance is not just a nasty habit that needs to be broken. It could all very well be a weapon in the enemy's arsenal that he is using to sidetrack you from hearing God's voice of direction and seeing your prayers answered. That leads me to our next treasure that awaits you in your bedroom—dreams.

Dreams—Your Bedroom Is God's Conference Room

I am going to let you in on a little secret. I don't know what your favorite part is about your relationship with God, but mine is how He communicates to me through dreams. Simply put, I love God's voice. I love hearing from Him and receiving His instruction while I am merely resting. I love hearing from God any time of day, but there is definitely something extra special about awakening—after a dream—to a life-changing revelation that resets the course of your life. Or at least the course of your day.

There is no way an imposter could call me and trick me into believing he is my husband. Likewise, there is no mistaking a "pizza dream" for the voice of my heavenly Father. I know His voice, and I know how He communicates to me in my sleep through both words and images. As I said, it is my most treasured part of my relationship with Him. But it was not part of my walk with God until 1993, when I received what Scripture calls the baptism of the Holy Spirit. By then, I had been enjoying a vibrant personal relationship with Jesus Christ for seventeen years. Yet I do not remember any significant or regular prophetic dreams coming until 1993, when I began to cry out in my prayer times for more of the Holy Spirit.

I have been sensitive to the voice of God since I was a very young girl. But in the late 1990s, I went through a "hearing drought" in which one stream of communication with God ("hearing" His voice) dried up and another started flowing all around and through me ("seeing" His voice through dreams and visions). And now, for almost three decades prophetic dreams have become such a regular part of my Christian experience that it has created a beautiful culture both within my family and within the church we pastor in Nashville, Eastgate Creative Christian Fellowship. Before our six children moved out and began building their own lives, breakfast table conversation always predictably contained the words, "I had a dream last night. . . ." We would run our dreams past each other for interpretation, advice and prayer. It still happens almost every single day, but of course it is either by text or phone call, or by one of them stopping by to get an interpretation from Mom.

As a family, we enthusiastically subscribe to the words of Job 33:14–18:

> For God speaks in one way, and in two, though man does not perceive it. In a dream, in a vision of the night, when deep sleep falls on men, while they slumber on their beds, then he opens the ears of men and terrifies them with warnings, that he may turn man aside from his deed and conceal pride from a man; he keeps back his soul from the pit, his life from perishing by the sword.

And this is not only part of our family culture. It is also part of the culture at Eastgate, where we carve out time during each week's Sunday service for an "open mic" segment in which, as our worship time is coming to an end, people are allowed to come share a prophetic dream, vision or word with the church. First, they run it by me on the front row to make sure it is something that would edify the Body of Christ. If so, they release it publicly for that very purpose.

With childlike faith and the foreknowledge of how God repeatedly spoke to His children through dreams and visions in the Bible, you can trust that a newly released dream or vision is like good seed in fertile soil. Then revelation springs forth and gives birth to application. This process should be a very natural and effortless part of your communication process with your heavenly Father. As I always say, *as His child it is your birthright to hear His voice.* Remember John 10:27: "My sheep hear my voice, and I know them, and they follow me."

In chapter 4 ahead, we will examine what a powerful weapon prophetic dreams can be in your life. As we just read from the book of Job, during a dream and a vision of the night, as you are in deep sleep and slumbering on your bed, God can open your ears to warn you and stop you in your tracks, turning you from the direction in which you were headed—thus saving your soul and sometimes your very life. Who in his or her right mind would refuse such information about tomorrow's activities, travels or business dealings? That would be like refusing intelligence information on the battlefield; you would be a fool!

> "I sleep, but my heart is awake; it is the voice of my beloved!"

Do not refuse it. Ask the Holy Spirit to remind you nightly that even just one solid prophetic directional dream from Him is worth making the trip down the hall and to your bed each evening. You never see anyone in Scripture begging God for a dream, but I don't think there is anything wrong with devoting your sleep to Him as you crawl into bed each evening and pray a simple prayer in keeping with Song of Solomon 5:2 (NKJV): "I sleep, but my heart is awake; it is the voice of my beloved!"

This is the main purpose of prophetic dreams. They are a direct pipeline to heaven's wisdom. They are not a badge or some mark of Christian maturity, and it does not take a supernatural deposit of faith to put stock in them. It merely takes the faith of a child to believe, receive and act upon a prophetic dream, whether it comes to you or through someone else for you.

Let me give you one example. In 2017, I posted on social media about how thankful I was to be almost done with the Quiet Brain patenting process. I believe we were also celebrating the one-year anniversary of the oil blend going to market. Out of nowhere, James Goll, a good friend, respected prophet and fellow Chosen author, left a comment on social media sites that there were "two new aromas/scents coming." It was a prophecy for all the world to see, and while you'd think I would have been happy with a word like this, all I could see was that I had just pushed one baby out and was being told that I was about to have two more. The patenting process had been so tedious, and I had done it in a matter of months, when it usually takes years to accomplish. I was also writing the patent myself since I really did not have the $20,000 to spend on a patent attorney.

Shortly after this, James also had a dream where he saw us getting a distribution process in place for all of these oils, and he saw a business emerging. So I had a choice to make—dismiss his word and dream, or get to work. James and I have a running joke that whenever he gives me a prophetic word, it usually involves hard work. I mean *hard* work. But that is okay since the words he has given me have been among the most rewarding of my life, once fulfilled!

I applied childlike faith to all of this and asked God for two new oil blends. You must understand that I am neither a chemist nor a lover of science. And I cannot bake a cake even with a recipe, so I meant it all three times when I asked God for the recipes for these three oil blends. I assure you that it is only my love of helping people that propelled me forward into asking God for these aromas. In no time at all, Happy Brain® and Sharp Brain® were created, trademarked and added to the patent before its submission.

In early 2019, I received word that the USPTO had awarded me a patent for all three neurological oil blends: Quiet Brain, for relief in the fight against insomnia, migraines, anxiety, tremors, seizures, ADD, ADHD, PTSD and more; Happy Brain, for combatting depression, lifting mood and suppressing appetite to assist with weight loss; and Sharp Brain, to aid in overcoming cognitive memory loss, concentration issues and focus deficits. But it all started with a word and a dream and some childlike faith. Yes, it involved work, but now those three little oil blends have become a bona fide business that has thrust me into the oil industry and has created a thriving company and ministry, Neuromatics Oil.

The moral of this story is that faith without works is dead, so be ready and listen for the Lord's direction in your life. Watch especially for prophetic dreams you will have, or that others will have for you—and quickly let your faith put feet to them.

These three treasures we just looked at inside your bedroom—peace, sleep and dreams—are just the beginning of what awaits you at the end of each workday, as you make your way to your bedroom and begin your nightly trip toward revelation and restoration. Do you remember your next steps as you go on from here? As I said in chapter 1, you are really only done with each chapter after you answer the questions at the end. This is a vital step toward revitalizing your sleep health!

Again, answer the following questions and save them for when you finish the book. At that time, use today's answers for Day 2 of my "10 Days to a Lifetime of Deeper Sleep and Dreams" program at the close of chapter 10. At the end of that day, a link will be provided that guides you to a good-night video where I pray a blessing over your sleep and dreams.

QUESTIONS AND PRAYER

1. What are three things you can change in your bedroom that will bring it order and peace?

2. Name a past dream that you think may have been prophetic direction from God, and if you did not act upon it, state why:

Pray this out loud: *O Lord, I need my bedroom to be an inviting refuge. Please help me to declutter it so that I might declutter my mind, and for me to be disciplined in treating that environment like the sanctuary it is. Bless my sleep each night so that I might navigate through each sleep cycle with perfect rhythm, resulting in having and remembering the prophetic dreams and guidance you want to bring me as I rest. Amen.*

THE MONSTERS
IN YOUR CLOSET

Remember when you were a kid and you would lie in bed in your dark room and imagine scary monsters and other entities hiding just out of sight in your closet? It not only kept you from going to sleep, but you also wondered how long it would take them to emerge once you finally overcame your fear and drifted off.

I was not given to fear as a little girl, but I can remember experiencing this a few times very vividly. There must be a large chunk of the population who share this fear, since Disney Pixar capitalized on it and produced the 2001 movie *Monsters, Inc.*, which grossed almost $600 million at the box office. This Academy Award–winning film introduced us to an entire hidden world of monsters that generates energy by scaring human children, despite the fact that the movie is a comedy. Kids are supposedly toxic to the monsters' plans for world bedtime domination, and everything goes awry one night when a child ("Boo") sneaks into the monster factory and two sympathetic monsters must return her by morning.

Obviously, as adults we have overcome our fear of monsters in our closets. Or have we? At some point in our lives, all of us have lain awake at night with worries about how we botched today's opportunities or with fears about tomorrow's looming tragedies. The vicious anxiety/insomnia cycle will not just go away on its own. You must be proactive and fight it as aggressively as it fights you, whether it nags you once a month, once a week, or every time you lay your head on your pillow.

Indeed, there are entities hiding just out of your sight—not necessarily in your closet, but in the wings of your life—and you know what they are. If you are a child of God, then His enemies are your enemies, and His enemies are set on destruction. They lie in wait for you to open the door to fear, and the reason they strike at night is because they know that is the time when you are vulnerable, quiet and more easily influenced. They generate energy by scaring humans, just like the monsters in *Monsters, Inc.*

So there you are, all snug in your bed, trying to drift off to sleep, and these enemies get busy whispering their deceitful intimidations to you. Lies about your family, lies about your job, lies about your church, lies about your health, lies about your future and even lies about your self-worth. Must you fall victim to this every night, or is there something you can do? I believe that if you will be brave enough to open wide the closet door and walk straight into the monster factory, you will find that you are not afraid of them, but they are actually afraid of you! Your faith is toxic to them.

In all my decades in ministry, I have noticed three common "monsters" that want to intimidate people of faith and that specifically start growling at nighttime in an attempt to steal our peace, our sleep and then our dreams. They are monitoring spirits, and some of those are familiar spirits, and all of them want you to dress yourself in garments of fear, worry and other equally disruptive and devastating things. I want to help you clean out your closet and deal with these monsters one by one so you can start to get a better night's sleep and take back your peace. Are you ready?

Monitoring Spirits—Demons That Monitor Your Activity

Did you know you have an enemy who has been studying you your entire life? He is none other than Satan, the devil, once known in heaven as Lucifer. Perhaps you have doubted his existence in the past, but surely you can look around you in the world today and see that it is becoming his playground. The Bible tells us that, long ago, Satan rebelled against God and was forced to leave heaven. He took one-third of God's angels with him, and these once-angelic beings became demonic entities that still operate on the earth today.

The good news is that these demons did not marry and procreate on the earth to increase their numbers. Our angelic helpers still outnumber them two to one. But that does not mean these entities are not busy. They have plenty of assignments from their diabolical leader, and on any given day, you are one of their tasks. If you are a person of outspoken faith who is constantly growing into the image of Christ and taking ground for God's Kingdom in this earth, then you will most likely be on the to-do list of these fallen angels every day of your life. Just because you do not feel it does not make it untrue.

> Did you know you have an enemy who has been studying you your entire life?

In fact, if you are an outspoken believer in Jesus and are not experiencing constant spiritual warfare, I can only attribute that to the fact that you are under the proper spiritual covering of the right pastoral leadership and/or that you have worked hard to close off every door and entrance point into your life. In effect, you have become invisible to your enemy. Yet even then, the enemy will push hard to reopen each door and rush in wherever invited—and sometimes where he is not invited!

Still, the enemy is smart. He has been around a long time and has these secret agents watching and monitoring you at all times. This is one of the reasons that I love Psalm 91 so much and claim it for my life. It begins by saying,

> He who dwells in the *secret place* of the Most High shall abide under the shadow of the Almighty. I will say of the LORD, "He is my refuge and my fortress; My God, in Him I will trust."
>
> Surely He shall deliver you from the snare of the fowler and from the perilous pestilence. He shall cover you with His feathers, and under His wings you shall take refuge. His truth shall be your shield and buckler. You shall not be afraid of the terror by night, nor of the arrow that flies by day.
>
> Psalm 91:1–5 NKJV, emphasis added

While I love the idea of dwelling in a secret place that makes me invisible to my enemy, the grueling truth is that I am human and often do things to run out from under God's refuge. Taking matters into my own hands, nursing that grudge, convincing myself that I am exempt from having to love the unlovely on any given Tuesday, et cetera, et cetera. And before I know it, I am no longer invisible *or* invincible.

The older I get, the more in love I become with quick repentance because of how it restores fellowship with God and gets me back into that hidden place where I am inaccessible to my enemies. Beware, because when you are accessible to your enemy—despite the fact that God's free gift of eternal life has secured your future in heaven—your life on earth can be very chaotic. Your enemy studies your frailties and is a patient investor. In fact, you may even see a pattern of how he tries to attack you with the same weapons over and over again. These are struggles with which you are so familiar that you can hardly remember life without having to battle them. Let me ask you these twelve questions:

1. Do your finances always seem to be lacking?
2. Do you often get injured or have accidents? (You are sick a lot.)
3. Do you struggle with a chronic ailment with little relief?
4. Do you experience unusual chaos and strife in your relationships?
5. Do you believe your marriage (or another relationship) is hopeless?
6. Do you ever think you might have bad luck or be under a curse?
7. Does prosperity seem to elude you?
8. Do you have a history of divorce or breakups?
9. Does it seem your promotions are always being sabotaged?
10. Do you ever doubt that God loves you?
11. Do you ever wonder if God even exists?
12. Do you notice history repeating itself in your family, with the same struggles surfacing from one generation to the next?

If you did not know what spiritual warfare is before, now you do. It is all of the above. And these are some of the many signs that a familiar spirit could be at work in your life. What is a familiar spirit? We will look at them closely and answer that question in the next section, because they are real. Identifying where familiar spirits are at work in your life will assist you in putting an end to needless and repetitious spiritual warfare.

But before we do that, I want to give you a scriptural example of a spiritual force that monitored someone. I believe these monitoring spirits are some of the "monsters in your closet." Acts 16 tells the story of Paul and Silas, as well as other believers, who were being followed by a spirit. I believe this spirit was monitoring their movements and reporting back to the enemy about the things they were doing, with the intent of bringing harm to their ministry. We refer to this type of spirit as a monitoring spirit.

> It happened that as we were going to the place of prayer, a slave woman who had a spirit of divination met us, who was bringing great profit to her masters by fortune-telling. She followed Paul and us and cried out repeatedly, saying, "These men are bond-servants of the Most High God, who are proclaiming to you a way of salvation." Now she continued doing this for many days. But Paul was greatly annoyed, and he turned and said to the spirit, "I command you in the name of Jesus Christ to come out of her!" And it came out at that very moment.
>
> Acts 16:16–18 NASB

The Bible says that this girl had a spirit of divination, which is the enemy's counterfeit of the prophetic gift. I believe she was monitoring Paul to gather information for her employers and not for her own use. Then it appears that she was reporting back to them with the information, and they would use it to plot against Paul and the others. This is exactly what "monitoring" spirits do. They have studied your comings and goings, your behaviors and habits, and they report them back to the devil, who has drafted a blueprint for the destruction of your family, career, happiness and future.

I am sure the owners of this slave girl with the spirit of divination were angry when Paul cast that spirit out of her. She was their slave no longer. She had to find a whole new job and start a whole new life. But she was free! And I am sure that the enemy is going to be angry when you dismiss the spirits that are tracking your steps each day to steal the future you are working toward, and that are trying to steal your health and divine instruction one peaceful night's sleep at a time. But freedom awaits you!

Familiar Spirits—Lifetime Monitoring Spirits

Let me start by saying this: All familiar spirits are monitoring spirits, but not all monitoring spirits are familiar spirits. In short, monitoring spirits are assigned to observe your actions, know how to push your buttons, watch for your weak spots, distract you and get you to quit or take a detour just before your prayers are answered. A familiar spirit does the same exact thing, but tries to attach itself to a family line for generational destruction.

Decades ago, prophet Bob Griffith visited the church I attended at the time and introduced this topic of familiar spirits to me. He said, "Just look at that word . . . *familiar*. It's the *family liar*!" The end goal of a familiar spirit is to derail you entirely from the calling of God upon your life, and to do the same in the lives of your children and grandchildren.

I love the way Missionaries of Prayer, an interdenominational network of Christians committed to praying, sums it all up in an online informational page about prayer against these types of spirits:

> The enemy has been studying you since you were born and these familiar spirits and monitoring spirits are there to check the status of your life and make sure that you never fulfill the purpose and plan that God has for your life. None of these spirits can actually read your mind, since God is the only one who is omniscient, so they can only gain information by watching you or hearing it from you or others around you. [1]

Their page goes on to say that if you keep experiencing the same problem or cycle of problems, almost like déjà vu, it is quite possible that a monitoring spirit is watching you and interfering with your life. A familiar spirit from your family line, for example, could be instrumental in making sure that your life is defined by the same struggles as your father and his father and his father—what is called a generational curse. But you can break all of this off! Just as Paul put a stop to the monitoring spirit that was interfering with him through that fortune-telling young girl, you can put a stop to this kind of enemy activity, too. In fact, says the Missionaries of Prayer page, "you must put an end to this if you plan on fulfilling your purpose and stopping a cycle in your life." [2]

> The end goal of a familiar spirit is to derail you entirely from the calling of God upon your life, and to do the same in the lives of your children and grandchildren.

Now let me provide you with my own practical definition of a familiar spirit, which I gave during a sermon I preached recently at Eastgate:

A *familiar spirit* is a monitoring spirit of demonic origin, assigned to you, your family, your group or community, and its job is to get to know you, lure you, attack you, then comfort you . . . then lure you, attack you, and comfort you again, all leaving you stuck in a vicious cycle in order to rob, kill and destroy your life. You are the only one who has the ability to open the door to allow this familiar spirit to minister to you in this way, and you are the only one who has the ability to close the door to it through prayer and repentance. It is never too late to be free of a familiar spirit.

I am now going to give you nine examples of what the Bible calls "familiar spirits" (all taken from the King James Version). The first mention of these spirits is found in Leviticus 19:31, which warned that God's people were not to consult with mediums or fortunetellers: "Regard not them that have familiar spirits, neither seek after wizards, to be defiled by them: I am the LORD your God."

The second example is in Leviticus 20, where we see in verse 6 God's opposition to His children's involvement with people who communicate with evil or familiar spirits: "And the soul that turneth after such as have familiar spirits, and after wizards, to go a whoring after them, I will even set my face against that soul, and will cut him off from among his people." And again in verse 27, it says, "A man also or woman that hath a familiar spirit, or that is a wizard, shall surely be put to death: they shall stone them with stones: their blood shall be upon them."

Deuteronomy 18:10–11 contains a third mention of familiar spirits, stating, "There shall not be found among you any one that maketh his son or his daughter to pass through the fire, or that useth divination, or an observer of times, or an enchanter, or a witch. Or a charmer, or a consulter with familiar spirits, or a wizard, or a necromancer."

Fourth is 2 Kings 21:6, where King Manasseh's reign was described as evil: "And he made his son pass through the fire, and observed times, and used enchantments, and dealt with familiar spirits and wizards: he wrought much wickedness in the sight of the LORD, to provoke him to anger." In a fifth example, the same details are mentioned about him again in 2 Chronicles 33:6.

Consulting evil spirits was listed alongside witchcraft and child sacrifice. During King Josiah's reign, he got rid of such evil practices. In a sixth example, 2 Kings 23:24 outlines his sweeping reforms that included removing those who consorted with familiar spirits:

> Moreover the workers with familiar spirits, and the wizards, and the images, and the idols, and all the abominations that were spied in the land of Judah and in Jerusalem, did Josiah put away, that he might perform the words of the law which were written in the book that Hilkiah the priest found in the house of the LORD.

Examples seven and eight are two mentions of familiar spirits in the book of Isaiah. Isaiah 8:19 says, "And when they shall say unto you, Seek unto them that have familiar spirits, and unto wizards that peep, and that mutter: should not a people seek unto their God? for the living to the dead?" God called His people to consult *Him*, not other spirits. Then Isaiah 19:3 adds, "And the spirit of Egypt shall fail in the midst thereof; and I will destroy the counsel thereof: and they shall seek to the idols, and to the charmers, and to them that have familiar spirits, and to the wizards." God made no apologies for the judgments that would come upon those who communicated with familiar spirits.

It is clear to see here that the term *familiar spirits* is used in connection with someone who utilizes or consults evil spirits. In each of these cases, the familiar spirit's goal was to take down an entire nation. You might say, "But I don't consult with evil spirits! I'm not a witch, nor do I practice divination!" But what if you *are* consulting with familiar spirits and don't know it? Look again at the first part of my definition of a familiar spirit:

> A *familiar spirit* is a monitoring spirit of demonic origin, assigned to you, your family, your group or community, and its job is to get to know you, lure you, attack you, then comfort you . . . then lure you, attack you, and comfort you again, all leaving you stuck in a vicious cycle in order to rob, kill and destroy your life.

Have you ever found yourself in such a vicious cycle? Are you sometimes tempted to partake in a certain behavior, attitude or activity, and after doing so, you feel so guilty that you allow the accompanying familiar spirit to stay by your side, actually bringing you a sense of comfort? This is the typical mode of operation of familiar spirits. They know what you are lacking. They know whom you are missing. They know what you like to eat, drink, watch and listen to, and they will try to gain access to you through all of these predictable habits.

Even right now, chances are very good that you know exactly what the familiar spirits in your life are. And if you do not, as you seek God He will show you. But if you do know what they are and can even see where you have been tolerating them in your life, then I must boldly ask you, as any good friend would: *If you know what they are and you know they are not God's best, then why do you continue to consult with them, entertain them, listen to them and obey them?* There is a better life for you—a life free of all familiar spirits, behaviors and unholy attitudes that separate us from the Holy Spirit.

It could be that, somewhere in the recent history of your life, you have become disfellowshiped from God. He has created all of us to need comfort. In fact, one of the names for the Holy Spirit is the Comforter. But the farther away from the Holy Spirit we get—which happens when we add unholy practices to our lives—the farther out of earshot we get from God's voice. We no longer feel His shining warmth on our faces, and unless we can train ourselves to connect our sin and lack of peace quickly to this disfellowship, we will begin to turn to counterfeits to find comfort. And trust me, one of these monitoring spirits that is familiar with your movements—and even its influence on them—will be waiting right there with a basketful of counterfeits for you to choose from. But in this chapter (and particularly in the next section), you can learn what the familiar spirits are in your life and family as we talk about this more.

I have noticed through all my decades of ministry that most people are consulting with at least six familiar spirits. Once they become aware of these spirits and receive deliverance, however, they will never again fall prey to their companionship or influence. Yet before we take a look at the top twelve familiar spirits I have encountered during my years in pastoral ministry, let's look at one more example in Scripture. Were you counting before? I only gave you eight examples, but I promised you nine. This final one mentions a familiar spirit five times. You have probably read this story before, but I hope that in these pages you are about to read it with new eyes and gain a revelation that will empower you to overcome these familiar spirits we are describing.

Now Samuel was dead, and all Israel had lamented him, and buried him in Ramah, even in his own city. And Saul had put away those that had familiar spirits, and the wizards, out of the land. And the Philistines gathered themselves together, and came and pitched in Shunem: and Saul gathered all Israel together, and they pitched in Gilboa. And when Saul saw the host of the Philistines, he was afraid, and his heart greatly trembled. And when Saul enquired of the LORD, the LORD answered him not, neither by dreams, nor by Urim, nor by prophets.

Then said Saul unto his servants, Seek me a woman that hath a familiar spirit, that I may go to her, and enquire of her. And his servants said to him, Behold, there is a woman that hath a familiar spirit at Endor.

And Saul disguised himself, and put on other raiment, and he went, and two men with him, and they came to the woman by night: and he said, I pray thee, divine unto me by the familiar spirit, and bring me him up, whom I shall name unto thee.

And the woman said unto him, Behold, thou knowest what Saul hath done, how he hath cut off those that have familiar spirits, and the wizards, out of the land: wherefore then layest thou a snare for my life, to cause me to die?

And Saul sware to her by the LORD, saying, As the LORD liveth, there shall no punishment happen to thee for this thing.

Then said the woman, Whom shall I bring up unto thee? And he said, Bring me up Samuel.

And when the woman saw Samuel, she cried with a loud voice: and the woman spake to Saul, saying, Why hast thou deceived me? for thou art Saul.

And the king said unto her, Be not afraid: for what sawest thou? And the woman said unto Saul, I saw gods ascending out of the earth.

And he said unto her, What form is he of? And she said, An old man cometh up; and he is covered with a mantle. And Saul perceived that it was Samuel, and he stooped with his face to the ground, and bowed himself.

And Samuel said to Saul, Why hast thou disquieted me, to bring me up? And Saul answered, I am sore distressed; for the Philistines make war against me, and God is departed from me, and answereth me no more, neither by prophets, nor by dreams: therefore I have called thee, that thou mayest make known unto me what I shall do.

Then said Samuel, Wherefore then dost thou ask of me, seeing the LORD is departed from thee, and is become thine enemy? And the Lord hath done to him, as he spake by me: for the LORD hath rent the kingdom out of thine hand, and given it to thy neighbour, even to David: Because thou obeyedst not the voice of the LORD, nor executedst his fierce wrath upon Amalek, therefore hath the LORD done this thing unto thee this day. Moreover the LORD will also deliver Israel with thee into the hand of the Philistines: and tomorrow shalt thou and thy sons be with me: the LORD also shall deliver the host of Israel into the hand of the Philistines.

Then Saul fell straightway all along on the earth, and was sore afraid, because of the words of Samuel.

1 Samuel 28:3–20 KJV

In his desperation to protect God's people, King Saul sought help from a medium so he could summon the spirit of Samuel for help during this difficult time for Israel. The result was a judgment that soon took the life of Saul and his sons. Note that instead of a familiar spirit appearing to Saul, it was actually the prophet Samuel. The medium typically consulted with a familiar spirit, so Samuel's appearance seemed to take her by surprise. And Saul thought everything was okay, until God rejected him because of what he had done. God's directive was clear—not to consult with mediums and the like (see Leviticus 19:31).

This is important because there are so many people who pray to their dead relatives and regularly pursue conversations with them. If heaven is a place of constant praise and worship to God, where there is no sickness or pain—which it is—why would your dead relatives be coming back to visit with you on earth? There is no evidence in Scripture that shows that Christians who have gone home to the Lord return to speak with their relatives. Maybe people who speak with their dead relatives are not actually speaking to relatives, but instead to demons. God may allow you to have a few dreams about a relative who passed on, but you should not be seeing that relative making appearances in your home. This could be a familiar spirit seeking to befriend you.

Many Christians do not believe that the psychic realm exists, but I assure you it does. This scriptural story of King Saul and the medium who summons the prophet Samuel is proof! Many psychics *can* predict the future and do consort and consult with familiar spirits. These psychics that you see on television, who deliver messages to audience members from their dead relatives, are a prime example. Recipients of these communications cry after hearing a message supposedly sent to them by "a loved one from the other side." The details are often so accurate that it leaves the listeners with their jaws dropped! How did the psychic give these people such accurate and comforting information?

Very simply, that psychic is consulting with a monitoring spirit that was on the scene when the deceased person was alive on earth. The spirit was an eyewitness to that person's life and can actually give factual information about it. But everybody gets their power from somewhere, and the power the psychics are summoning here is diabolical and dangerous. At the end of these psychics' earthly lives, thousands of evil spirits will be fighting over the ownership of their souls. At the end of my life, there will be just one Spirit

> At the end of my life, there will be just one Spirit present to claim ownership of my soul—the Holy Spirit. I pray that the same can be said of you, my friend.

present to claim ownership of my soul—the Holy Spirit. I pray that the same can be said of you, my friend.

If you have never heard the testimony of someone who once consorted and consulted with evil spirits, I want to give you the opportunity to do so right now. Earlier I referenced a sermon I recently preached at Eastgate Creative Christian Fellowship, the church Chris and I pastor in Nashville. I invite you to listen to it. It includes the testimony of a former psychic/warlock and the encounters he had with these easily summoned spirits. Watch the video sermon "Stuck" at https://youtu.be/6l8z1kUmb9E. (The time frame that includes his testimony starts at 55:33.) It is part 1 of our entire multi-video series called "Unstuck" that we preached in October and November 2020. In November 1's video, Chris does a great job of further defining familiar spirits. He teaches from James 1:6–8, which says of anyone asking God for wisdom,

> But let him ask in faith, with no doubting, for the one who doubts is like a wave of the sea that is driven and tossed by the wind. For that person must not suppose that he will receive anything from the Lord; he is a double-minded man, unstable in all his ways.

Chris explains that the compound word *double-minded* is actually the Greek word *dipsychos*. In addition to its more traditional definitions, this word also means "two spirits" or "two-spirited."[3] This is the perfect picture of the internal war experienced by an individual who is trying to be led by the Holy Spirit, but is being held back by a familiar spirit. If you have been feeling unable to make progress—as if you are stuck physically, emotionally or spiritually—then there may be another spirit besides the Holy Spirit that is trying to guide your life. Let's take a closer look at that possibility next.

A Wardrobe to Die For—Cleaning Out the Closet

Up until now, I have described the monsters in your closet as spirits and diabolical forces. Monsters indeed! Who would want to sleep in a room with a closet full of spirits? But what if I told you that these spirits looked less like gremlins, goblins or Gollum from J. R. R. Tolkien's *The Hobbit* and *The Lord of the Rings*, and more like the attitudes and behaviors you put on each day? In the same way that you get up every day and go to a closet full of familiar clothes to decide what you will wear, each day you are presented with opportunities that cause you to choose what type of attitude, reaction or expression you will have. What are you more likely to do when presented with an infuriating situation at home? Do you (a) reach for the jacket of anger that you can slip on with hardly a moment's notice, and readily vent your frustrations, or (b) reach for the warm, fuzzy sweater of love and put it around your adversary's shoulders, thawing his or her frigid expression and heart of ice?

I daresay all of us have a jacket of anger that gets more wear than it should. We would rather patch its elbows and ignore its nasty stains than reach for the lesser used and more beautiful sweater of love. Why? Because the angry jacket is more familiar. Both will make you warm, but the angry jacket is faster to put on. It has a quick zipper, whereas that sweater of love has at least a dozen buttons. Putting on that sweater seems too hard, too slow and too much a waste of time, so you whip the angry jacket off its hanger instead, and off you go to wear it for the rest of your day. This is really no different than what it feels like to slip on or slip into consulting with a familiar spirit.

Do you remember the little girl, Boo, who upset the whole monster factory when she walked into it by accident in *Monsters, Inc.*? Well, I am going to ask you to walk into your emotional closet on purpose right now—the monster factory of all of your feelings and reactions—and take a look at your "psychological wardrobe," especially the most familiar items that show the most wear. These are what your family and closest friends most often see you clothed in. These are how you choose to "bare" your soul, but in this case, *BARE* is an acronym for your *B*ehaviors, *A*ttitudes, *R*eactions and *E*xpressions.

As I said before, I find that if left unchecked, most people will be in constant consultation with at least half a dozen familiar spirits in their lives. These spirits are as close to you as the thoughts in your mind and the conversations that occupy your thoughts, and they hope to influence your every move. Here are twelve such spirits (or groupings of spirits) that I have noticed most often in my decades of ministry. Satan uses all of these to manipulate God's people and keep them out of His will for their lives. See if any of these are in your monster closet:

1. *Fear* (asks, "What if I fail or am put to shame?")
2. *Rejection, Abandonment* (says, "Nobody loves me.")
3. *Anger, Hate, Bitterness* (says, "I cannot stand him/her. I am done.")
4. *Anxiety, Worry* (asks, "What if . . . ?")
5. *Doubt, Unbelief* (says, "Nothing good can happen for me. God must not want it.")

6. *Loneliness, Isolation, Suicide* (says, "I am all I have, and I'd rather be dead.")

7. *Insecurity, Low Self-esteem or Self-worth* (says, "I do not deserve any better.")

8. *Pride* (says, "I know that I'm right and you're wrong.")

9. *Passivity, Spiritual Apathy* (says, "I've got all of the Holy Spirit that I need.")

10. *Lust, Perversion* (says, "I can't stop until I have what I want, even if it's wrong.")

11. *Unforgiveness* (says, "I will never forgive them. I deserve to hold this grudge.")

12. *Unholy Compromise* (says, "It's just one time or one tiny wrong concession; it won't not affect my overall faith.")

These all compose the wardrobe and vocabulary of the world, do they not? They should not be part of your vocabulary as a child of God. Make no mistake, they are sins. But the analogy of describing them as clothes helps you begin to notice when you are choosing these things from your spiritual or emotional wardrobe, and it helps you instead begin choosing a different Spirit to be clothed in—the Holy Spirit—your Helper.

If any of the aforementioned things are a regular and familiar part of your behaviors, attitudes, reactions or expressions, today is the day for you to clean out that closet. I would like to lead you in a prayer to accomplish that.

But first, here are four steps for you to take before we pray, and they replace the usual two chapter-end questions:

1. On a separate sheet of paper, list any negative thoughts or emotions you have on a regular basis. Those are your familiar spirits. Familiar spirits generate feelings and, as established,

often run in families. The more you allow them to speak to and through you, the more they will occupy your life and your legacy. Familiar spirits are both demanding and comforting, and if you continue to tolerate them, they will hide from you what God calls sin, and you will never feel as if you are in close fellowship with God.

2. Ask yourself for an opinion of yourself, if that makes sense. Proverbs 23:7 (NKJV) says, "For as he [actually, anyone] thinks in his heart, so is he." Luke 6:45 (NKJV) talks about what comes out of a person's heart:

> A good man out of the good treasure of his heart brings forth good; and an evil man out of the evil treasure of his heart brings forth evil. For out of the abundance of the heart his mouth speaks.

So take a few moments and identify the good and bad that you and others see in your heart and that make you who you are.

3. Contemplate if what you are battling is a monitoring spirit that is merely trying to ruin your day or a familiar spirit that is trying to destroy your family. Think about the patterns of spiritual warfare that accompany these forces and see if they predictably strike at a similar time. Perhaps you feel loneliness and have suicidal thoughts at the same time each night. Perhaps you will experience family strife just before each and every Christmas gathering. These spirits desire to create problems in your life. They know the misfortunes and the generational curses that plague your family, and their goal is to create cycles and seasons of destruction in your finances, business, body and future. If you see a pattern of a time of year or time of day that the spiritual warfare regularly manifests, make a list and become proactive in prayer before it has a chance to catch you off guard the next time.

4. Look at your list from #1 that identifies any familiar spirits in your life and see if you can remember when they first began communicating to you (when these emotions and reactions first began manifesting). Perhaps it was after a trauma in your life—whether physical, emotional or spiritual—or maybe after you opened a door and walked headlong outside the will of God and into sin. Try, if you can, to link memories and see if you can find the origin of the entrance point of each familiar spirit (unhealthy familiar emotions and activities).

Now that you have identified the familiar spirits in your life through our list of twelve, or through others we may not have named, and now that you have contemplated their entrance points and cycles or seasons, I am going to lead you in a prayer of deliverance. It is very important that you pray the prayer before another night passes, so I am going to also include it here. Again, I urge you to watch the "Stuck" sermon I preached at https://youtu.be/6l8z1kUmb9E. Just as I was finishing reading this list of twelve of the most familiar spirits during the sermon, I looked up from my notes and did a bit of a double take—which you can see in the video at 2:14:49—because about 80 percent of the church was already at the altar (or spilling into the aisles). They were coming for deliverance. They were coming to trade in all of their familiar spirits for the Holy Spirit. They were coming forward for a divine exchange. I invite you now to do the same thing. You can pray the prayer along with me in the sermon video at the end of the message there, but let's start here (it is a bit different), and then in chapter 4 we will further investigate the power of prayer.

You will need to pray this out loud to combat the spiritual attacks against you. The demonic realm must hear the authority in your voice, and the familiar spirits must know that you mean business as you clean out the emotional monsters in your life that are causing you so much spiritual harm and even physical damage.

Pray this out loud: *Dear God, I don't want to have "two spirits." I want to be guided only by one Spirit, Your Holy Spirit. Right now, as I think back over my life, my actions and my choices, I know I need Your forgiveness. I'm sorry for the way I have given another force the right to influence my actions and words. I receive Your forgiveness, and I also offer forgiveness to those people who have influenced me to behave in this way. I pray that they would find the relationship with You that they need to gain victory over negativity and sin. Use me to help them, while also sending more positive influences into my life, beginning with people who are full of Your Holy Spirit.*

I close every door I have opened to the familiar spirit of _____, and I ask right now to receive grace to resist it, should it ever come knocking again. Familiar spirit, you are dismissed. Fire of God, consume my enemies. I bind and restrict any familiar spirit from my life, no matter if it was invited or uninvited. In Jesus' name, I declare from this day forth that I hear only the voice of the Holy Spirit. I will allow only Him to guide my steps. I decree freedom over myself and call for an end to repeated spiritual warfare and seasonal struggles in my life. I cancel the plans of the enemy, which he has drafted for my destruction. Hallelujah!

I ask God to commission warring angels around my home for protection, and also inside my home to minister to me right now. Today is a new day. I am covered. I am loved. I am connected to the Body of Jesus (the Church) in a new way, and I expect to prosper in all things and be in good health, even as my soul prospers. Every obstacle that has stood in the way of God's calling on my life is now crumbling in front of me, and a path is being cleared for promotion and joy. I receive healing right now—body, mind and spirit! No more delays! No weapon formed against me will prosper!

I thank You, God, that You have preserved my life, and that You are also giving me patience today as You pick up the pieces and work all things for my good and my bright future. Today I receive this salvation, my calling and purpose, and this deliverance, in the name of Jesus. And now, I invite in the place of familiar spirits the Holy Spirit, for He is the only Spirit I want occupying my heart. Holy Spirit, I invite Your holiness into my life, my speech, my media, my playlist, my refrigerator, my vocabulary, my thoughts and my bedroom. In Jesus' name, Amen!

These four steps and in-depth prayer take the place of your typical chapter-end Questions and Prayer section. But refer back to them on Day 3 of my "10 Days to a Lifetime of Deeper Sleep and Dreams" program at the close of chapter 10. At the end of that day, a provided link will guide you to a good-night video where I pray a blessing over your sleep and dreams.

I want to end this life-changing section with a poem I wrote that you can also declare over yourself:

> Rescue me, O great God, and set me free
> Liberate my captive heart of its chains
> You are the only One who has its key
> I am the only one who feels its pains
>
> At birth my heart was whole, my spirit too
> But one by one the tribulations came

And on their heels came grief before I knew
Then I was left with bitterness and blame

You've saved my spirit; now please save my mind
Erase the fears the years have nursed and fed
Repair the built-in trust that's been maligned
Replace it with salvation in its stead

There are no tactics left to see me through
Deliverance can only come from You.

© Laura Harris Smith, April 9, 2015

THE WEAPONS
UNDER YOUR PILLOW

Let's say you prayed that important prayer from the previous chapter to rid your life of all monitoring spirits, familiar spirits and any spiritual force that is trying to steal tomorrow's blessings from you—starting with tonight's good night's sleep. What do you do if you lie down at night and these monsters are still growling at you in the dark?

What if you cannot get today's failure out of your mind? What if fear is getting the best of you, or if you are staring at an obvious rejection? What if you are still angry, even though you have prayed and forgiven? What if you are struggling to move past anxiety, worry, doubt and unbelief so you can start again tomorrow? What if you are lonely, suicidal or struggling with lust? What if you are insecure and just don't want to go on? And what if you feel that pride or unforgiveness still nips at your heels, or that spiritual apathy still plagues you after an unholy compromise?

Very simply, it is time to slip your hand under your pillow and take advantage of the weapons waiting there for you. These weapons make up a powerful arsenal that includes your dreams, your prayers and your rest. You do not have to lie in the dark and worry. You do not have to stare at the ceiling and rehearse something you wish you had done differently. You do not have to toss and turn. Remember, you are fighting for your sleep because you are fighting for your health, but you are also fighting for your dreams because, as we established before, they are your direct pipeline to heaven's wisdom. Let's start right there, with your dreams, as we consider the arsenal at your disposal as you lay your head on your pillow each night.

Dreams—Solving Your Problems While You Sleep

Did you know that if you were to do a topical study on dreams, you would learn that one-third of the Bible is about dreams and visions, or about the result of a dream or vision? That is amazing! To exclude dreams as a viable source of direction from God is like existing on two-thirds of a healthy spiritual diet. Furthermore, it puts you in danger of committing the Revelation 22 sin of "taking away" from Scripture (see verse 19).

No, your dreams are not Scripture, but they definitely can be scriptural. We see all throughout the Bible where God uses dreams and visions to communicate with His people. In fact, in Scripture there are 21 dreams that came from God to an individual who was at a crossroads and needed direction. Among all of these dreamers, two are named Joseph, six are kings, and only one is a woman. I would like to outline the dreams in Scripture for you here so you can get an idea of how God likes to communicate with you to keep you from harm and heartache. What He did for those in Scripture, He will do for you. All you have to do is be in a relationship with Him to be able to hear His voice. Remember the Job 33:14–18 passage we first read in chapter 2? Let's take another look at it, and I think it is even a good idea to commit it to memory:

> For God speaks in one way, and in two, though man does not perceive it. In a dream, in a vision of the night, when deep sleep falls on men, while they slumber on their beds, then he opens the ears of men and terrifies them with warnings, that he may turn man aside from his deed and conceal pride from a man; he keeps back his soul from the pit, his life from perishing by the sword.

Now take a look at this list of the dreams God sent people in Scripture:

1. Abimelech's warning dream in which God stops this king from sleeping with Abraham's wife, Sarah (see Genesis 20).
2. Jacob's ladder dream where he sees angels ascending and descending upon the ladder stretched from heaven to earth (see Genesis 28:12).
3. Jacob's instructional dream where God tells him to return to his father's land (see Genesis 31:10–13).
4. Laban's warning dream from God to release Jacob to return home (see Genesis 31:24).
5. Joseph's dream of eleven sheaves of grain bowing down to his one sheaf, foreshadowing that his brothers would one day bow down to him (see Genesis 37:1–8).

6. Joseph's dream of the sun, moon and stars bowing down to him, also signaling that his father and brothers would bow down to him (see Genesis 37:9–10).

7. The Egyptian cupbearer's dream about pressing grapes into a cup and giving the drink to Pharaoh, showing that the cupbearer would be restored to honor (see Genesis 40).

8. The Egyptian baker's dream about carrying a basket of bread for Pharaoh on his head; the bread gets eaten by birds, revealing that the baker would be executed (see Genesis 40).

9. Pharaoh's dream of seven fat cows being swallowed up by seven thin cows, portending seven years of a coming famine in Egypt (see Genesis 41).

10. Pharaoh's dream of seven plump stalks of corn being swallowed up by seven thin stalks, again foreshadowing seven years of a coming famine in Egypt (see Genesis 41).

11. The unnamed man's dream of the loaf of bread that rolls into the Midianites' camp and turns over their tents, foreshadowing a victory for Gideon (see Judges 7:13–15).

12. Solomon's dream where he is offered anything by God; he chooses wisdom and is given everything as a result of this wise choice (see 1 Kings 3:5–15).

13. Nebuchadnezzar's dream of the great statue made of diverse materials that represent future empires; it is crushed by a stone symbolizing God's Kingdom (see Daniel 2).

14. Nebuchadnezzar's dream of a magnificent tree that is chopped down level to the ground, representing the fall of his great kingdom and his coming years of insanity (see Daniel 4).

15. Daniel's dream about four beasts that represent four kingdoms—a lion, a leopard, a bear and a mysterious creature with ten horns—and how they are judged by God as of the Son of Man is given dominion (see Daniel 7).

16. The carpenter Joseph's dream where an angel tells him that Mary is pregnant with the Savior of the world, Jesus, and not to be afraid to take her as his wife (see Matthew 1:18–24).

17. The magi's warning dream for them not to return to Herod after finding the babe in Bethlehem, thus protecting the Christ child (see Matthew 2:1–12).

18. Joseph's dream in which an angel tells him to escape Herod's slaughter of all male babies in the area by leaving for Egypt immediately with Mary and the baby King (see Matthew 2:13–15).

19. Joseph's dream in which an angel tells him that it is safe to return to Israel now that Herod is dead (see Matthew 2:16–21).

20. Joseph's dream about avoiding Herod's son, who now sits on the throne in Judea (see Matthew 2:22–23).

21. Pontius Pilate's wife having a nightmare about an innocent man—Jesus—being condemned to death (see Matthew 27:19).

These 21 dreams all came to sleeping individuals; otherwise, they would have been visions. (Although number 15 in this list, from Daniel 7, is referred to as both a dream and a vision, depending on your Bible translation.) Of course, visions in Scripture are too many to number if you count them all from Abraham, Jacob, Joshua, Moses, Balaam, Elisha, Micaiah, David, Job, Isaiah,

Jeremiah, Ezekiel, Daniel, Amos and Zechariah. And those visions are just in the Old Testament! In the New Testament, we see visions from Zechariah, John the Baptist, Peter, James, John, Paul and of course John the Revelator, whose 22-chapter book is one long vision!

God was talking back then and He is still talking now, protecting His children. Guiding them, as He did Israel, through the desert with a cloud by day and a pillar of fire by night—except in this case, He is guiding you with His voice by day and dreams by night. And here is some even better news: According to Acts 2:16–18, where Peter quotes the prophet Joel, we are on the verge of a worldwide intensification of this type of dream activity. I see evidence that it has already begun!

> But this is what was uttered through the prophet Joel:
> "And in the last days it shall be, God declares, that I will pour out my Spirit on all flesh, and your sons and your daughters shall prophesy, and your young men shall see visions, and your old men shall dream dreams; even on my male servants and female servants in those days I will pour out my Spirit, and they shall prophesy."

This is happening, and you need only jump on board in faith and become part of this sensory revival. God loves to talk to His kids. If you have kids, do you like to talk to them? Sure you do, and you miss them when that communication wanes. It is the same with God your Father. In *Seeing the Voice of God*, I outlined ten types of prophetic dreams, defining them and showing how they can be used for prayer and direction. You can read the biblical and personal examples I gave of each of those types there, along with what each type of dream requires of you when you have it. Here, however, I want to outline for you some new examples of dreams I have had from God. It might work differently for you, but I would like to let you step inside my visual relationship with the Lord by seeing four of the dream types in action. I will start with two examples of dreams that are for "now"—*waking dreams* and *encouraging dreams*.

Waking dreams

There is no mistaking a waking dream because it becomes the very first thought of the day for your yet unused mind, and the first conversation you have with yourself. Dreams you have just before waking up stay with you all day like a pesky friend, unlike those dreams you have in the middle of the night and forget by morning. I advise you to pay close attention to your waking dreams because God saves them for the last few minutes of your sleep for a reason. They are going to require action, maybe even that very day.

For instance, this last Sunday I awoke to a dream that I was leading a team with football plays, and the very last play was that we would not use our young MVP quarterback. The dream defied logic, but that is what we knew had to happen, and it did. When I awoke I was greeted by my husband, who told me that our son Jhason—Eastgate's associate pastor—would be unable to preach that morning as scheduled (monitoring some cold symptoms in an abundance of caution). So it would fall upon us at the last minute.

I laughed out loud in response, mainly because God had placed me in this dream as a sports coach, something I have never done, nor want to do. But I also laughed because I was not using these football plays on a football team, but on a deliverance team (a group of people who convene to pray in agreement for a specific outcome regarding a person or urgent situation). Since our nation had had a particularly divisive week, with the results of a presidential election hanging in the balance, we turned that service into a time of prayer for our nation's deliverance from all corruption and confusion.

While I normally don't like to get up and preach with no preparation or prayer, this encouraging dream showed me that it would be okay. And it was encouraging to my son Jhason to know that God thought of him as our young MVP quarterback!

Another example of a waking dream occurred on the morning of Jhason and Brittany's wedding in 2013. My daughter Jeorgi was eighteen and had a friend named Donovan who was two years younger. He was a good friend of Brittany's, too, and had traveled a thousand miles from Minnesota to be an usher in their wedding. I woke to a dream where I was asking Jhason, "Do you think that Donovan is Jeorgi's future husband?" and Jhason answered, "Yes. Yes, I do."

I woke up so stunned! I knew that they had once had a bit of a crush on each other, but it had not been sustained over the thousand-mile distance, so I was tempted to dismiss the dream. Yet since it was a waking dream, and since, more often than not, that meant God needed me to do something with it the same day, I asked Him for two confirmations: *God, if Donovan is Jeorgi's future husband, then I need You to (1) have Donovan be the usher who walks me down the aisle as the mother of the groom, and (2) work it out to where I can get a quality picture with him.* If he was going to be my future son-in-love, then I wanted to document this important family day and make it memorable, especially since I had no idea when I would see him again.

As it turned out, it would be another six years! But that is exactly what God did for us that day. In fact, He combined my requests, and I have a beautiful picture of Donovan walking me up the aisle. And although Jeorgi is very much a prophetic dreamer, the dream would have confused her during those years when she

> I was thankful I had documented the dream
> from years before—which prophesied him as
> her husband—and had sealed it in an envelope
> for the day of their wedding. There was
> hardly a dry eye or a closed jaw in the whole
> reception hall as I read it to everyone.

and Donovan lost touch, so the Lord would not release me to tell her the dream. I wanted to so much because I knew it was a prophetic dream, but I also know that in matters of love, it is always best for a prophetic mother to allow her children the blessing of discovering that love for themselves, which is what I did. I did tell Jhason and Brittany the dream, however, and as suitors came and went over the years, we would pull out the dream and pray with it.

Six years later, Donovan reentered Jeorgi's life, and the very next summer they were married. My reception speech as her matron of honor was to read this amazing prophetic waking dream to them for the first time. I was thankful I had documented the dream from years before—which prophesied him as her husband—and had sealed it in an envelope for the day of their wedding. There was hardly a dry eye or a closed jaw in the whole reception hall as I read it to everyone. The dream was a combination of a waking dream and an encouraging dream, which is next up on our list.

Encouraging dreams

You will know you have had an encouraging dream from the Lord when you want to stay under the covers, shut your eyes, go back to sleep and keep dreaming it. But of course, since encouraging dreams are in the "now" category (although they can be for now or later), they often make me eager to jump out of bed and watch them play out in the very near future!

Speaking of Jeorgi's wedding, we were in the final stretch of preparations right as all the biggest bills were coming due, including the wedding gown. Then I had a dream that I was making the dress myself (which would be a disaster!) and piecing it together with materials from here and there. I didn't even tell Jeorgi the dream and still have not (surprise, Jeorgi!) because I knew it would actually *discourage* her, seeing as I can hardly even sew on a straight button. Plus, Jeorgi had already had an encouraging dream that she had won a wedding dress, so I did not want to contradict that hope. I think by that point, she had also stumbled across a wedding gown giveaway online and had registered for it, but a long time had passed and many people had entered, so I further felt that my dream would seem to cancel hers out. I said nothing and just prayed.

Lo and behold, about a month later a bridal shop contacted Jeorgi and told her she had won! The prize was only for a $1,000 dress, and there was another one she really wanted that was a bit more. But by this point the Lord had also fulfilled my dream that He would increase oil sales in my online store and increase my book sales, too. Piece by piece, He put together the funds for us to buy Jeorgi the exact dress she wanted. It was the fulfillment of two dreams in one—mine and hers—and we both remember the goodness of the Lord every time we see the pictures of her in her wedding dress.

My favorite dreams of this nature are those that I get to deliver to other people, brightening their days with hope, if needed. As a pastor, God gives me plenty of these for my congregants, and I love making that phone call or sending that text message with an encouraging dream for someone. It helps people keep going and makes all the difference between giving up and rising up.

I have lost track of the babies I have seen in dreams—little ones who have finally come to the couples I submitted the dreams to, including my own adult children and their spouses. Earlier this year, I dreamed that my son and daughter-in-love, Jhason and Brittany, would have a second child who would be spaced the exact distance from their first child as Jhason was from his sister Jeorgi (in other words, my closest two). Within weeks, we got the news of their baby number two being due at that exact time, spacing the siblings precisely the same number of months apart. You might wonder why our kids would be encouraged about possibly having two in diapers for a short time, but when you wait as many years as they did for miracle baby number one, you welcome another one and really appreciate the advance warning on timing!

Always make sure you have a solid interpretation before approaching someone else with any dream, however, because without that, an encouraging dream could quickly turn into a discouraging one. For example, one day my very good friend and prophetic intercessor Sue Teubner called me and said, "Laura, I dreamed last night that Eastgate was two churches, and I was coming to visit."

My heart sank because the term *two churches* summoned thoughts in my mind of a church split. When I pressed her for details, Sue said, "No, no, no! I was visiting the second service just as the first service was letting out. Two services, not two churches!"

We got a good chuckle out of that, especially me since our church was nowhere near the place of needing to go to two services at the time, since we had not yet been in our new building for very long. Add to that how the pandemic of 2020 tried to empty out churches everywhere, and I wondered how on earth that dream would ever come to pass. But here we are in 2021, facing that very decision as Eastgate Creative Christian Fellowship has grown and multiplied. Praise God for Sue's encouraging dream that we grabbed hold of and prayed about until we saw it come to pass!

Now let's take a look at some examples of two types of dreams that are sometimes "for later"—*warning dreams* and *directional dreams*.

Warning dreams

A warning dream is one that contains information that may be a little unsettling or alarming, but its purpose is to alert you and prepare you for the upcoming situation, conversation or even battle. Many people mistake warning dreams for nightmares because they see something in the dream that might make people fearful or uneasy. But with proper prayer, a warning dream is just that—just a warning—and its contents will never come to pass, because your prayers will thwart the plans that the enemy was drafting against you.

The majority of warning dreams I have are for my children, but that is because I have six kids and they are such world changers! Plus, I pray fervently for them, and when you do that, God will speak to you about the people you pray for. But I do not tell my children every little warning dream I have for them, because some of the dreams are just assignments for me to pray. With the Spirit's prompting and timing, I share the dreams I feel are the most urgent or helpful. How thankful to God I am for this type of dream that alerts you and me about oncoming spiritual warfare. With proper examination, prayer and discernment, such dreams help us overcome it.

God also saves me a tremendous amount of time and energy with warning dreams that He gives us as pastors. I once had a *warning waking dream* (a real double whammy) that Chris and I were walking peacefully by a river and that suddenly a snake started chasing us. But this was not just any snake. It had a large head that was a man's head, with a human mouth, and it had a body at least twenty feet long. I watched this snake emerge eerily from the water, slither up onto the bank and come toward me at a speed too great for me to outrun. I actually outran Chris, but on looking back over my shoulder, I saw that the snake had bypassed him altogether and was coming straight for me. I knew that if it caught me, it would entangle me and squeeze me to death. I also knew that my only defense was to get to higher ground. I saw a tree just in front of me and felt confident that I could climb it.

I awoke from the dream just before I saw the outcome. I awoke very alarmed as well, especially at the scary sight of the snake's human head and mouth, but the Lord told me very quickly what it meant. Even before I was out of the bed, He told me to prepare myself for a verbal assault on us as pastors by one individual. This verbal assault would very quickly single me out and attack just me, but I was not to become entangled by it. I was to get to higher ground, where I could stay safe.

Within hours all of the dream came to pass, and I did indeed feel as if I were running for my life, or at least for my reputation. This assault included negative and false talk about us to many people in the church. One by one, they began approaching us to try to confirm it. We wound up having to go to each member—house by house, family by family—to undo the lies. To suck out the poison from the snakebite.

We had to engage in quite a bit of communication to clean up the confusion, but just as in my dream, I never became entangled with the person behind it. We did, however, have to ask him to leave the church, based on Titus 3:10, "Warn a divisive person once, and then warn them a second time. After that, have nothing to do with them" (NIV). This person had been lovingly warned over the years about how his words had repeatedly caused destruction in one situation after another. After he had met one final warning with absolute vitriol, we told him we loved him, but that for the sake of the church we were going to have to cut ties. Many other church members did the same thing once they saw him take to Facebook with his grievances. Even when grievances are warranted (which these were not), it causes intense damage to the Body of Christ to be so publicly divisive. So we said our good-byes. Then, wondering what I could do to go even higher, as I had seen myself doing in my dream, I reached out one more time and all but begged this person to please let our most precious moments together be what we remembered about each other. The response was more negativity and anger, so—feeling as though we had been obedient to God in going above and beyond what He would require—we walked away. But it all started with that one morning dream that helped guide my every footstep that week.

> Isn't God good? Through warning dreams we can outrun the enemy and win the battle!

The pastoral cleanup took more than a month to bring truth and total vindication, but we never had to deal with that spirit itself again. God had shut the jaws of death. And not only that, but real church growth started immediately after that person left. Backbiting left, gossip left and a critical spirit was nowhere to be found. We entered into the most peaceful days we have ever experienced at Eastgate, as evidenced by the fact that we were soon bursting at the seams in our new sanctuary. Isn't God good? Through warning dreams, we can outrun the enemy and win the battle!

Directional dreams

A directional dream is just that: It provides you with direction you did not have before. I remember several years ago dreaming that my son Julian was going to sell his house. In the dream, I was telling him that he should not sell it. I submitted the dream to him, and sure enough, he and his wife, Sarah, told me that they had been considering the same thing. When they needed to move out of state shortly after that, they decided not to sell the house, but to rent it. On the day they were packing to move out, I dreamed that they were back and living in the house again, and Julian was in his early thirties. I did not tell them this dream because I thought it would be discouraging to be packing up all of your belongings with the knowledge that you were just going to have to move back and unpack them one day! Yet sure enough, that is exactly what they did just after he turned thirty.

As far as receiving direction for myself in a directional dream, I remember that immediately after inventing Quiet Brain oil, I had a dream one night in which I saw oil flowing out of bottles. I was so excited, feeling as if the dream symbolized the anointing, or maybe a new flow of income. While both of those things did come to pass, so did something else. Our very first hurdle as a company was when our rollerball bottles began to malfunction. Customers were complaining that the bottles leaked, and even worse, that they were arriving almost entirely spilled out. Suddenly, my directional dream took on new meaning and I knew I had to get to work and find a better bottle supplier!

Another example of a directional dream took place when I decided to go back to school after the age of fifty and become a nutritionist. I learned so much and did so well that the founding doctor of the institute I attended told me I would be a prime candidate for their doctoral program. I had to think long and hard about pursuing three degrees at my age—finishing my bachelor's, attaining my masters in Original Medicine (Christian body, mind and spirit medicine), and then earning my doctorate in the same. I really needed God to give me direction!

Then a woman in Atlanta whom I had never met, Pastor La-Ronna Turnbough, tracked me down to invite me to speak at the church she and her husband, Otha, founded and pastor. In her email was a directional dream for me. She had dreamed that I was a naturopathic doctor. I could hardly believe it! And then another confirmation came: I myself dreamed that I was speaking to a large audience and looked down and realized that I was hardly dressed. I was embarrassed and left the podium long enough to go find more clothing. The only clothing I could find, however, was a white doctor's coat! I put it on, returned to the podium and felt incredibly confident. When I awoke, I knew I had the confirmation I needed. Yet a final confirmation came that next month, when God provided a large check made out to us. It paid for all three of my degrees upfront. I paid the schooling off in full and began my steady uphill climb toward fulfilling this directional dream.

I also find that my son Jude is in a lot of my dreams. Decades ago, I began realizing that sometimes you need to look at the people in your dreams not as participants, but as people whose names bear some significance to the scenario you are dreaming about. The name *Jude* means "praise," so when I see him in a dream, I always know that I am to praise God regardless of the situation, and that it will work out to my advantage as I give God praise! My daughter Jenesis is also in my dreams a lot, and *Jenesis* means "new beginnings." I am always encouraged when I see her in a dream, and I feel God is directing me to prepare for something new. My other four kids are not left out, either. *Jeorgi Anna* means "industrious in prayer," *Julian* means "youthfulness," *Jhason* means "healing" and *Jessica* means "wealth." It never ceases to amaze me how all six of my kids show up at just the right time . . . both in my life and in my dreams!

Prayer—Training Your Inner Intercessor to Engage

Now that I have given you examples of the different types of dreams—some that are for now and some that are for later—let's discuss what happens in that period of time between your dream and its fulfillment, should the process take longer than you expect. It can feel like that awkward stage you had back in junior high, when you were trying to figure out where you fit socially, who you wanted to be to the world, and what you were saying to yourself on the inside. You were so busy trying to master all those things and were so emotionally close to the process that you thought you looked perfectly fine on picture day . . . until the pictures came back and you were forever documented in an embarrassing annual that you hoped would never see daylight.

It is the same way with a true prophetic dream about the future. You begin thinking and planning, combing over every inch of it with a fine-tooth comb, becoming convinced along the way of what it means. Then you start telling other people about it, and whether they ever say it or not, you can tell that they think you are crazy. In fact, if you are honest, you sometimes look back on how you interpreted a dream and laugh at yourself, just as you laughed at that awkward-stage photo.

The thing is that our first response to a prophetic dream should never be "thinking and planning." It needs to be "praying and waiting." If you know that a waking dream is for right now and you must take action immediately, you can at least still pray and have

God birth an interpretation in you. If time is short, He will speak clearly and quickly. If you do not do this, you might get ahead of Him and make a big mess you will have to clean up.

I cannot believe this nutritionist is about to give you this example, but here goes: If the prophetic dreams you have at night are like a stack of flapjacks, then prayer is the syrup to your every pancake. Never take a fork (thinking) or a knife (planning) to them before flooding them with prayer. Eating pancakes without syrup is like eating a loaf of bread dry; they will just stick to the roof of your mouth. Acting on a prophetic dream without prayer is likely to be just as sticky and difficult to swallow. (And now that you want pancakes, but also want to think about your health, try HighKey gluten-free pancake mix, topped with SweetLeaf sugar-free Stevia syrup. You're welcome.)

So it matters not whether you are a prayer veteran or a prayer rookie. If God gave you a dream, then He will give you the grace to pray it forth (or to thwart it if it is a warning dream). The following steps will help you get focused with your prayers. I put the steps into an easy-to-remember acrostic for you that spells (of course) *PRAYERS*. As you begin praying, make sure that you are ready to . . .

Participate. Remember our key verse: "The effectual fervent prayer of a righteous man availeth much" (James 5:16 KJV). Understand that God needs you to engage with Him without distraction.

Receive revelation. Paul prayed "that the God of our Lord Jesus Christ, the glorious Father, may give you the Spirit of wisdom and revelation" (Ephesians 1:17 NIV). Understand that prayer is a two-way conversation. Allow yourself time to listen and receive revelation from God about how you should pray or interpret your dream.

Agree. "If two of you on earth agree about anything they ask for, it will be done for them by My Father in heaven" (Matthew

18:19 NIV). Be willing to agree with God on the direction He gives you. Get confirmations from your spiritual leaders if you are unsure.

Yield. Paul also said, "Wherefore be ye not unwise, but understanding what the will of the Lord is" (Ephesians 5:17 KJV). Be willing to submit your will to God's will when in prayer. If you feel prompted to pray, then pray. If you feel prompted to listen, then get quiet. If He tells you to go to the Word, then grab your Bible and yield to wherever He nudges you to read.

Enforce. "How happy are those who enforce justice, who live righteously all the time" (Psalm 106:3 ISV). Remember, you are an enforcer, not a beggar!

Roar. "Sound your battle cry" (Psalm 68:30 NET). Pray out loud. God does not require it, but your enemy needs to hear it—and so do you. If you feel yourself becoming impassioned as you pray, flow with the Spirit and let Him pray through you.

Spirit pray. Jude tells us that as the beloved, we are to be building ourselves up in our "most holy faith and praying in the Holy Spirit" (Jude 20). Pray in your prayer language. This is a topic we will cover more in chapter 8, and I can *hardly wait!* This is a key component in knowing how to pray when you can find no revelation to do so, or when you are trying to interpret a dream.

And let me just add extra *emphasis* to the third step, *Agree.* The word Jesus used for *agree* in Matthew 18:19 literally means in the Greek "to agree with one in making a bargain, to make an agreement, to bargain; to stipulate (by compact)."[1] That word *compact* is another word for a "contract," and *to stipulate* means "to demand." And when Jesus says, "anything they *ask* for," that Greek word for *ask* means, among other things, "to call for; with the idea of demanding prominent."[2] And here is where it gets good! What all of that reveals is that when Jesus tells you, "If two

95

of you on earth agree about anything they ask for," He is actually instructing you to go find a friend, and then He is giving you both permission to "put a demand upon His contract with you," which He fully intends to honor! It is not as if you are placing a demand on God; you are placing a demand on the contract He provided, which are the promises in His Word! And the Greek word used for *thing* in the same verse literally is defined as "a deed."[3] As you know, a deed is a legal contract that transfers power and promised possessions from one party to another. So if you will think of your Bible as the legal deed that outlines the power and possessions promised to you, your prayers will come from a place of authority. You have bargaining power with God, so put it to good use!

I find that as I begin to do these things in prayer, my prayer time takes off. Morning, afternoon, evening and, yes, even at midnight. I have friends who do not like to pray in bed because they get sleepy when they pray, or some of them are married and do not wish to wake their spouse. But I have single friends who love to go to bed and spend an hour or two in the dark, just praying out loud by the Spirit's leading. Guess what: If you are having trouble falling asleep, this is a great way to start downshifting after you finish those "hot and glowing" fervent prayers.

Now let's look at some other practical ways to help you catch more ZZZs.

Rest—Getting to Sleep and Staying Asleep

Working with so many people who are not getting the rest they need, in the amounts they need, prompted me to come up with some way to help them that would *work*. The result of my efforts is what I call my "ABCs for ZZZs," a list in which I outline some practical, concrete steps you can take to get a better night's sleep.

Unless you have a major underlying health issue, this list will work for you so well that you will be amazed. I have taught on it before and even included it in one of my other books in similar form, but I also want to provide it for you here:

A. *Abstain from all caffeine, nicotine and alcohol since they can lead to insomnia.* Caffeine lurks in many things besides coffee, like chocolate, soft drinks, nonherbal teas, diet pills and energy drinks. And for deep sleep, skip the nightcap since alcohol can help people get to sleep, but won't let them stay there. And smoking is bad for both your lungs and your sleep cycles. Your sleep will vastly improve if you will rid your body of such habit-forming, life-altering substances. You may have purchased this book in the hope of better sleep, without knowing that we would address the hazards of some of the evening comforts you enjoy. But I assure you that they are no match for the type of rest and dreams the Prince of Peace provides for you, so it is an easy trade.

B. *Bedtime Math.* What time must you awaken in the morning? Subtract at least 8 ½ hours from that time to determine your bedtime. That allows 8 hours of actual sleep time, preceded by 15 minutes to wind down (doing these ABCs for ZZZs) and 15 minutes to actually fall asleep. If you need to rise at 6:00 a.m., then be in bed no later than 9:30 p.m. (Adjust these times to fit your schedule.) Try to reach step C on this list 15 minutes before bedtime each night.

C. *Create room atmosphere and temperature.* As you begin your descent toward bedtime, use soft lighting to begin adjusting your circadian rhythms. This will signal your brain to pump out the "drowsy juice," melatonin. Cool down the temperature a little bit from the daytime (so you are neither too hot nor too cold during sleep), and perhaps turn on a fan for some white noise.

D. *De-stress for 5 minutes before climbing into bed.* Sleep is a sacred time, so create some of your own bedtime traditions. Essential oils on your pillow are good, or you can use a warm face wash or take an Epsom salt bath (the pure magnesium sulfate aids sleep). Establish some kind of favorite relaxation routine to train your body that sleep is near.

E. *Enter.* Now it is time to transition into your bedtime clothes, bedroom and bed itself. Lie down, close your eyes and enter into peace. Ask God to enter your dreams and speak to you in the night.

F. *Forgive.* Just as important as cleansing the atmosphere in your room is cleansing the atmosphere of your heart. That means forgiving whoever ruined your day or night (especially if it is the person lying next to you). What you go to bed with, you wake up with, so choose love. "Don't let the sun go down while you are still angry, for anger gives a foothold to the devil" (Ephesians 4:26–27 NLT). Also ask God to forgive you for whatever He brings to mind, and forgive yourself! Start fresh again tomorrow.

G. *Go to sleep.* Find your "sweet spot"—your favorite sleeping position. Try slowing down your breathing, which mirrors what happens in the early stages of sleep. Doing this basically tricks your brain into thinking you are there already, which causes your brain waves to slow down and widen.

(I have done this for years.) If sleep still does not descend, spend a few minutes writing in a gratitude journal, listing just three things you are thankful for. Or read for just a few minutes. Use an actual book, however, and not your Kindle, iPad, other tablet or iPhone, because the direct lights from those will cue your pineal gland to quit making melatonin and will wake you up. Finally, pray Psalm 127:2 over yourself: "For so He gives His beloved sleep" (NKJV). And remember, sleep is the mattress of dreams.

Go down the list of my ABCs for ZZZs for several nights in a row, establishing a bedtime routine that will soon change your sleep habits for the better. And something else you can add to your bedtime routine that was unavailable when I first came up with my ABCs list is the Quiet Brain oil I told you about in chapter 2. Every batch is created in a silent environment of prayer and worship. I think the miracles I hear about from people who have used this product have more to do with this spiritual factor than with the scientific factors of the healing power God put in each of its individual oils. I believe God is not just *in* Quiet Brain, He is *on* it.

Finally, if you still have trouble falling asleep after implementing this list, or if you are continually tired during the day, consider seeing a sleep doctor. It is all right to ask a good physician for help! Just remember to filter his or her wisdom through the higher wisdom of the Great Physician.

Again, answer the following questions and save them for when you finish the book. At that time, use today's answers for Day 4 of my "10 Days to a Lifetime of Deeper Sleep and Dreams" program at the close of chapter 10. At the end of that day, a link will be provided that guides you to a good-night video where I pray a blessing over your sleep and dreams.

QUESTIONS AND PRAYER

1. Name any biblical objections you have for dreams being used by God to guide you.

2. Name two changes you can make at night for a better bedtime routine.

Pray this out loud: *Holy Spirit, I need You to speak into the situations that trouble me. I believe You want to, and I ask You to show me how to better steward my evenings so that I might fall asleep, stay asleep and receive direction from You. May I better employ the weapons You have given me that are accessible as I lay my head on my pillow each night. As a result of increased prayer, may an intimacy with You translate into prophetic dreams that guide my path and bring me peace. In Your name, Amen.*

THE WORLD OUTSIDE
YOUR WINDOW

Sometimes you can create the perfect refuge in your bedroom, will yourself to bed and master all your monsters, yet you still cannot seem to get to sleep or stay asleep. The reason is that sometimes the chaos is not in your house or heart, but outside your window. I am not describing those pesky night sounds like sirens in the city or tree frogs in the country. I am talking about those things in the world that are entirely outside your jurisdiction or control. Things you see on the news. Things you read on your phone. Societal events of a community or political nature that inundate you with ultimatums, but never ask for your advice on them. Except for a trip to the ballot box every couple of years, these things leave you feeling helpless and sometimes even hopeless. Not only can they keep you up at night; they can also highjack your dreams and turn them into apocalyptic nightmares if you are not careful.

Ecclesiastes 5:3 describes how anxiety can cause restless dreams, so you never want to go to bed anxious. Take a little time to wind down using my ABCs for ZZZs from the previous chapter. Even then, most nights you will go to bed with your head full of current events, headline news, political drama and countless Facebook opinions about it all. I would like to devote this chapter to helping you refuse to allow this governmentally unstable world to steal your peace, sleep and dreams. In fact, I would like to teach you how to use prophetic dreams and prophetic intercession as a means by which to actually make our world more stable. And of course, once you see your prayers and dreams working together to accomplish that, you will begin to experience the sweetest and safest sleep you have ever had in your life.

I firmly believe that Holy Spirit prophetic dreams and Christ-centered prayers are the cure for every problem God's world faces. For every problem you and I face. The reason is that we are gaining wisdom from heaven with which to make choices that change our circumstances, and then we are partnering with God to accomplish it. Who would not find that appealing? I urge you really to wrestle with God over this truth, if necessary, and to camp out in this chapter until you are convinced of it.

My life has never been the same since I surrendered my sleep, dreams and prayer life to God. You should surround yourself with people who understand this truth so that you can begin to receive a steady flow of revelation, both from their dreams for you and yours for them. And it is especially cool when you see your dreams coming true for the nation or even the nations. The things "outside" your window—the political theatre in your dreams, the glowing stimulant of social media, and that little box, the TV, that brings the outside world inside—are no match for the steady flow of revelation that comes to you from the heavenly realm while you sleep. Let's look at how to put each of these areas to rest so that you can rest.

World War Me—Political Theatre in Your Dreams

More than twenty years ago, I had a dream during which I was asked if I would take a vow. I was in a cave and had been summoned there by the prophet Elisha. I waited nervously until I saw him enter with his servant—who I assume was Gehazi from 2 Kings 4 and 5—and then Elisha came and stood face-to-face with me. He asked, "Will you take a vow to pray for America?"

Without hesitation I answered yes, and then he motioned for me to drop to my knees. Using his staff, he placed it on my shoulder as if he were knighting me with a sword. He went through all the same motions, lightly tapping the staff on one shoulder, then over my head and on the next. I awoke and was blown away at what I had just experienced. It felt exactly as if I had knelt before Elisha and received part of his anointing. My thoughts raced in the following two directions.

(1) *Why Elisha? Why not Jesus?* I knew the story of Elisha well and that he was Elijah's eager young protégé who had asked for a double portion of Elijah's anointing. So I immediately knew that the promise of a double portion awaited me with keeping this vow. And I can attest to the fact that God has kept His end of the bargain by pouring out a double portion of anointing upon Chris and me greater than we ever could have imagined back when I had this dream, at a time while we were experiencing great lack and chronic sickness. We have doubled in business, doubled in ministry, doubled in family, and we even have a set of twin grandsons. While I would have loved for this dream encounter in the cave to have included Jesus, the truth is that I already have access to every

promise He provides. The presence of Elisha, however, alerted me that God was wanting to reward my obedience to pray with the double-portion blessing, which is what Elisha represents in Scripture since he was the one who asked for it (see 2 Kings 2:9–10).

(2) *I have just seen myself answer yes in a dream and make a vow that I assume I will now have to keep!* It reminded me of when God asked Solomon in a dream what he desired more than anything, and instead of riches Solomon chose wisdom, which God then told him was the correct answer. Then He wound up giving him both. There was no specific time requirement for these prayers in my dream, nor was it specified what their focus should be. It was just "pray for America." Since that time, I have indeed felt an increased burden to pray, an increased love for my country and an increased overall patriotism that has found its way into every area of my faith.

This dream and my yes have even changed the way I watch the news, insomuch as I feel less like a spectator and more like a participant, or even like a spy gathering wartime intelligence to take back to my commander in chief. Not that God doesn't already know the evening news, but He definitely wants it prayed about, and I am always eager to hear His opinion on man's report. Sometimes He agrees with it, and sometimes He does not. But every time, He shows me His perspective and how I can pray for His will to be done on earth as it is in heaven.

My journey of keeping this vow through the years has taken me to some interesting places in the middle of the night! I have had—in dreams—fascinating conversations with governors, presidents and even Martha Washington. Each dream comes with an assignment to pray for the individuals if they are still alive, or for their governmental legacy if they are not. Either that, or their presence in the dream is a little clue from God about something

---

I have had—in dreams—fascinating conversations with governors, presidents and even Martha Washington. Each dream comes with an assignment to pray for the individuals if they are still alive, or for their governmental legacy if they are not.

---

that might be coming down the pike for America, as it did in their administration.

I have always wondered if God tells these deceased leaders in heaven that He is using them and their lives on earth to offer direction for someone who will be interceding in prayer down on earth in the twenty-first century. Now, *that* is a conversation I would love to overhear since I have always been fascinated with the Hebrews 12 concept of a "great cloud of witnesses" watching us!

Nevertheless, I love my political dreams because after each one, I feel a deep sense of satisfaction that I am partnering with God to actually get something done on earth that needs doing. Sometimes a dream even leads me into assignments that bring me before government officials, which is when it really gets fun. But more often than not, I merely "see and release, see and release, see and release." Dream it, pray it and then watch it unfold later on the news. Mission accomplished.

During the twenty years since I had that dream with Elisha in which I vowed to pray for America, God has shown me who would win all the presidential elections, and the last two times He showed me in a dream. With Barack Obama, I had a dream on

Election Day in which I saw him emerge from Air Force One and wave to a crowd. He was colorfully dressed in beautiful African royal robes and smiling that winning smile, and I knew immediately upon waking that he would be the victor. I did not vote for him, largely because as a mother of six children—none of whom came at a convenient time—I cannot ever bring myself to vote for a candidate who is not pro-life. The morning after the election, however, I took to Facebook and congratulated him, called him "my president" and vowed to pray for him. And I most certainly have kept that vow with more fasting and prayer than I have ever put into any other president in my lifetime. I also went to see him when he came to town, taking my children along to teach them respect for the office of the presidency, and the importance of praying for the president.

In July 2016, I dreamed about the next president. I had been in fasting prayer all week for another matter, and I told God on going to bed that I was sorry I had been praying all week about my issues. Then I asked Him to please show me in a dream that night what He wanted me to "pray in." I told Him I would devote the rest of the week to it. The next morning as I was coming out of sleep, I had a waking dream/vision in which I saw Donald Trump being sworn in as the next president. He had one hand on the Bible and one hand in the air, and was on the Capitol steps, per tradition. It was a gray and rainy day, and I was positioned in the crowd to his left. I was stunned. This was not at all what I had meant when I had asked God to show me what to pray for. But I had made a promise to God, so I decided to begin to pray accordingly.

Months later I was invited to the Presidential Inaugural Prayer Breakfast, and my Democratic congressman made a way for me to attend the inauguration. To my absolute shock, when I arrived at the inauguration I was positioned exactly in the audience as I had been in my waking dream/vision. It had never dawned on me that I would be there physically. I just assumed that I was watching it happen in the dream, so you can imagine my surprise when we arrived and I was positioned in the crowd to the president's left, exactly as I had seen. It surely does bolster your faith when you experience such confirmations, and you build upon that faith one fulfilled dream at a time, while simultaneously experiencing the intense peace that comes from knowing you are within the will of God.

These are just some examples of how I have used dreams, prayer and words from the Lord to deal with the world outside my window. Doing the same will help you find peace, feel less fearful and not have to wait years to have your voice be heard at a ballot box. I love praying for my presidents and for all my government officials, and I can immediately spot a person who does not do so. How do I know? You cannot pray for your leaders privately and defame them publicly. Your heart develops sensitivity for those you pray for, and you lose all angry feelings and instead acquire the heart of God for each one of those individuals.

If you are having trouble finding peace with the world outside your bedroom window each night, start with prayer. Then watch your words during the day. Do not pray for peace, but then make war with your conversations. That includes social media posts and comments.

Since many people who struggle with sleep lie in bed and scroll endlessly through Facebook, Twitter and Instagram, I would like to devote the next section to helping you navigate through this very topic at this very time of night—not just because what you read in bed is important to your sleep health, but because how you respond is also important to your reputation. And to God's.

Social Media—The Glowing Stimulant

You are lying in bed, trying to sleep. You pick up your phone, go to your social media sites and start to scroll. Physically speaking, this is a bad idea because the glowing light hits your optic nerve and cues your pineal gland to cease melatonin production. Melatonin is the drowsy hormone, and without it you will never go to sleep. So the very act you are engaging in to get to sleep is actually stimulating you and preventing sleep.

I want to offer another suggestion: Put down the phone and pray for your nation. By laying down that device, you are signaling to God that you are willing to pick up the burden for your nation. Ask God to speak to you directionally as you sleep, and just start by praying for whatever is going on in the world around you . . . in the world outside your window.

Since 2020 was such a challenging year for the world, with a novel pandemic, and such a challenging year for America, with a divisive presidential election, I would be remiss if I did not give you an example of what I am describing, based on that season when so many Americans were bitterly divided. I decided to pray and do a partial fast for the 40 days before the 2020 election, and not just for its outcome, but so that I would be wise with my words and influence others the way God wanted me to. I prayed for 39 days before writing anything for social media, and even then, I did not post what I wrote until Election Day. I waited until I had two solid dreams that final week that I was convinced were from the Lord. But what I thought would just be a post about the election soon turned out to be a teaching opportunity about the power of prayer, as it pertains to prophetic dreams.

I also felt the need to leave my readers on social media at peace and gain their trust first, since they are people from both political parties and I was certain they would all be experiencing political-opinion fatigue by then. Here are some excerpts from that post, because it will help you understand how I combine prophetic dreams with prayer (and occasionally fasting) and accomplish great spiritual warfare with them, while entirely immersed in peace. I will also include interpretations of the dreams for you and how I arrived at them. Finally, all of this will also show you how to handle social media posts that marry religion with politics, which is usually the only way I ever post anything political.

But remember, try not to create posts like the following right at bedtime. Not only will the glare prevent you from ever getting drowsy, but the comments will also start pouring in, and you will be unable to resist reading them . . . the good, the bad and the ugly.

This post was from noon on Election Day 2020 (edited for publication here):

> I've lost track of the times over the decades that I've been told I should've gone into politics. I had an enjoyable brush with student government in school, and one of my first jobs in the early '80s was in politics, working in the campaign for the first woman to win election to a statewide office in Tenn. (a Democrat). Eventually my creative side won out for a career in media, and I have found that most of the production sets I visit are full of Democrats (all of the secular and a good number of the religious). Fifteen years ago my media career embraced ministry with the birth of Eastgate Creative Christian Fellowship, and of course now I have my own TV show and write books for those audiences. The cameramen I hire are both Democratic and Republican. My viewers are both Democratic and Republican. When I was growing up, my parents voted both Democratic and Republican, as did I for many years (something that's hard to do now). I taught my children to respect the president, and whenever one came to town—Democrat

or Republican—I packed the kids up and we went out and stood in the heat or cold and waved as he passed by and prayed for him. Both times I've been invited to the U.S. Capitol, it was by a Democratic congressman. I've been to one presidential inauguration, and it was for a Republican president. But the tickets came from my Democratic congressman, and I went to his office in D.C. to pick them up and say thanks. I would say that most of our Eastgate congregants are conservatives and many love Trump, but some do not trust him and did not vote for him.

All of this to say, it's not so easy for me just to spout my political opinions on social media without alienating someone I love. Yet as a leader and especially as a prophetic intercessor, I spend a great amount of time on my knees, seeking heaven's opinion about our earthly leaders and the raging of the nations, because it's critical. And I do not just pray and do all the talking. I start by listening, and then, by the Spirit's leading, I try to pray what God wants, keeping my mouth shut until I am sure (because prayer is *powerful*). I do find that the more time I spend in prayer, the more dreams I have of a prophetic nature through which God guides my prayers, and the more accurate they are and more they come true.

I did have a waking dream/vision in mid-2016 that Donald Trump would win and be sworn in as president on a gray, rainy day, and he was. I put that vision on Facebook in a non-partisan post (but still lost friends). So now, in this election, I have had people asking me if God has shown me anything again. Here is what I have to say on Election Day: No literal dreams this time about Trump winning, but if he is going away and losing the presidency, God has not shown it to me. I, like many of you, my Facebook friends, have spent the last 40 days in a time of extra prayer for our nation, something I chose to do because I was getting worried I was missing something in "the silence." Finally this week, two dreams came. Neither seems significant on the surface, but underneath, I believe they are.

Dream #1: It is March 2021, and I am on vacation with Donald and Melania Trump. In Florida. He is not in a suit and tie, but just casual attire, and he and Melania are relaxing in our shared condo and enjoying the beautiful view. The mood was peaceful and relaxed. Part of me wonders why he was in Florida in this dream and not in the White House, but perhaps it represents a season of rest coming for him after years of warring (and he is a Florida resident, technically). I also pray to God that the "March 2021" doesn't mean that it takes that long to count votes and decide the winner! But next, I saw the numbers "20–27" flash in front of the two of them. I'm still praying about what that means. I think I know (the years 2020–2027), but I don't want to engage in eschatological discussions in this post. It could be key electoral votes; we will see.

Dream #2: I was standing beneath two flagpoles, and the largest U.S. flags I've ever seen were hoisted above me and whipping in the wind. Massive, and I was bending my neck back trying to see them so high in the heavens. *In the dream* I felt this represented "2 terms" (for Trump), but *upon waking* I wondered if it symbolized the "2 Americas" we seem to have right now. A divided nation. But just like my 2016 rainy inauguration vision, and just like the sunny Dream #1 above, the weather stood out to me here, too. Behind the waving flags was a perfectly blue-sky day. So vivid, almost as if it were a picture in which God had enhanced the saturation for extra color. Not a cloud in sight. Happy, and *so much peace*. I felt proud to be an American standing there.

Wouldn't we all like that? Wouldn't you? Would that be okay with you, even if your candidate does not win? If you cannot say yes and pray for your president (despite party), then you don't have a president problem, you have a God problem. We must all learn to trust God more than man. And we must let our prayers change what legislation and civil disobedience cannot. Those 2 things can change a lot, but *not everything*. And just as we need 3 branches of government, we also need 3 components for cultural change in tumultuous times: legislation, *civil* disobedience, and prayer. So I have voted today, and with great confidence that I am being obedient to God with my vote. I am not voting for Donald Trump to be my pastor, my husband or even my teacher, but to be my president, and I will continue to pray fervently for him since he has the most impossible-to-please-everyone job on the planet (*besides* being a pastor). You may not like Trump's COVID response or his tweets, but if you are a Christian, surely you can see that He desires to protect Christians, Israel *and* the unborn, and you can get behind that. If you are not a Christian, perhaps you can see where the economy was going pre-pandemic and try to let Trump finish the job he started.

Bottom line of this long post is: *Pray for that sunny, cloud-free day for our nation so that every American can stand proud beneath the flag, look to heaven and be at peace. Please, God, heal our land.*

I am happy to say that I did not lose one friend after posting what you just read. In fact, I gained hundreds of them! In 2016, I did lose a few friends from my post mentioning President Trump's inauguration in a non-partisan way. But this time around, I feel that everyone could see my motive, which was to rally prayer with these dreams and not just spout forth political revelations. One reader whom I do not even know responded that my book *Seeing the Voice of God* should become core curriculum in schools and that college credit should be offered for completing it. Wow!

And then, lo and behold, Election Day came and went with no winner. Months would pass as we all sat on the edge of our seats . . . or knelt on our knees . . . waiting to hear of a winner. Certain news outlets called Joe Biden as the winner less than a week later, but the Associated Press did not call it for weeks. Newsmax never did during the entire saga. To my horror, I saw my dreams starting to make more sense, and I had a feeling that this could stretch out until early 2021. I lay flat on my face several times that election week and cried out to God to put a word in my mouth to encourage the American people, specifically the praying Church. In short, He told me it was time for mobilization and not encouragement. He wanted me to urge His people to pray, and it was all happening simultaneously as accusations came forth of fraudulent voting, additional voting, deceased person voting, ballot harvesting and manipulation of the main tabulation software.

Then one night I had the following prophetic dream: I was standing in a hotel lobby, so I assume I was traveling. I was looking up at a TV monitor in the corner, and some sort of decision or verdict was being issued from a high authority. I heard the decision and in the dream said, "Oh, thank God." I then started to cry out of one eye. Only the left eye was crying. The next night, I had another dream that an "exposure of corruption" was also going to find its way into the Church. That very week, a prominent pastor was fired for moral failures, and I sensed that this was just the beginning of how far the exposure of corruption and dishonesty would reach. I also heard of and was given the opportunity to speak directly and pray with another worship leader who had confessed to occasional drunkenness and a pornography addiction.

I did not release that last "Oh, thank God" dream in writing on Facebook, because I felt God's prompting instead to schedule and advertise a Facebook Live broadcast in which I would discuss all the prophetic dreams I have shared with you, along with a very strong word He was giving me for America. Here was His simple word: *I am extracting corruption out of your political system . . . and I am extracting prayer out of My Church.*

I exhorted everyone from 2 Chronicles 7:14, "If my people who are called by my name humble themselves, and pray and seek my face and turn from their wicked ways, then I will hear from heaven and will forgive their sin and heal their land." Once again, the response was overwhelming, and 99.9 percent positive. And even the .01 percent negative responded positively to my soft reply to a negative comment. We had thousands of viewers and rallied an army to pray.

Yet still, I would go to bed each night and beg God to give me more so that I could rally better prayer for America. Finally one night in early December 2020, I dreamed that author and international speaker Pastor Dutch Sheets said firmly to me, "Well, if you're going to beg God, release it!"

I woke up and knew why God had used Dutch to say this. At the time, Dutch was heavily involved in traveling to all the battleground states that had come under question due to suspected voter fraud, and he was leading prayer meetings in each one. But I could not understand how God could think I was not releasing these prophetic dreams and words, since I was doing so regularly on Facebook through my extensive Facebook Live videos.

Then it hit me: *I have a TV show.* How had I forgotten that? So we quit doing the livestreams on social media and in December 2020 we dedicated all of season 5 of *theTHREE* to America, the election crisis, praying for our government officials and more. We called the season "America the Beautiful," and the response was overwhelmingly positive. It was neither Republican- or Democratic-targeted, but focused entirely on governmental prayer and prophecies. Our viewer mail more than quadrupled in response. I felt that my urgency to release these prophetic dreams to the public was finally satisfied, and I used this medium to do so, while also releasing the prophetic dreams and words of the prophets internationally. (You can view those shows at www.theTHREE.tv.) It was glorious!

In January 2021, even with a new presidential inauguration under America's belt, two of my prophetic dreams about the election stood out as being yet unfulfilled. Not wrong—just hanging out there, seemingly unanswered. They required more prayer, more fasting and more patience, as sometimes your dreams will. They were both one scene each, yet combined, they left me with a ferocious burden in prayer. One was the dream where I was traveling and saw on a lobby TV monitor some sort of verdict coming down about the 2020 election (which I assumed was from the Supreme Court or another branch of government), and where I exclaimed the words, "Oh, thank God" and began to cry. The fact that I was crying out of only my left eye led me to believe that whatever this news was, it would not please "the left," the Democrats. The other mysterious dream was the one about relaxing on vacation with the Trumps in Florida in March 2021, while seeing the numbers 20–27 flash before them. What did it all mean?

Since both dreams involved travel, and since we were indeed planning to be in Florida in March for our anniversary, I decided to move the trip up a week so that we would actually be there on March "20–27," just in case the dates were significant for coinciding with the other dream about being in some sort of hotel or public lobby and seeing that shocking verdict on a TV monitor. I had no other trips on the books for early 2021, so I assumed that this trip was my one shot at seeing these dreams fulfilled during it. The date change was a simple act of faith. It was all I had to contribute as I waited and prayed. (And we wound up staying both weeks!)

By the time we got to March and were packing for Florida, where Trump was now living, he had survived two impeachments via Senate acquittals, and he had begun to reemerge on the public scene. The April 4, 2008, prophecy from Kim Clement had also been re-released by his ministry through his daughter, Donné Clement Petruska,[1] since he had gone on to be with the Lord days after Trump was elected in 2016 (an election outcome he had also predicted years prior). Here is that April 4, 2008, prophecy verbatim (italics added):

And they shall say, "but now there is a second President, how can we have two presidents?" *An usual thing, isn't it?* says the Spirit of the Lord. . . . "We have two presidents. What do we do now?" Fear not, for God said, *as I promised before, this is My Nation and I will change things according to the time and season and I told you now in Spring I will expose and reveal things that have been hidden.*"[2]

He prophesied this on the same night:

I feel the Spirit of the Lord telling me to tell you: There is a reason to have joy at this moment—for many say, "this is the worst time ever in America." . . . God said, *this is the best time, because joy is coming to you in the Spring,* says the Lord, *Joy is coming to you in the Spring, therefore, I want you to prophesy it: Joy!"*[3]

Christians, non-Christians, prophetic types and those skeptical of the prophetic were still all abuzz trying to interpret this "Spring" prediction at the time of our trip, which began on the first day of spring.

I decided that while in Florida on vacation, I would do a partial fast and pray for our nation without the distractions of work back home. One viewer of *theTHREE* had written to say he felt that in my dream I had shared on-air about Trump being there, relaxing in the condo with us during these key dates, my presence represented all the intercessors who had prayed so faithfully and fervently about the 2020 election (who now needed to rest). So with them in mind—which may very well include you—I also decided to pray for *you* while on this much-needed vacation. I prayed for God to reward you and all governmental intercessors in a very tangible way, starting with giving you His peace. Should nothing change on our national scene, and should these dreams of mine hang out there for another time or another year, you would need that peace all the more.

While Chris and I were in Florida, some key events took place. First, more than one major national magazine and newspaper published articles giving credence to the fact that the 2020 election had not gone smoothly at the ballot boxes and that it looked as though some serious reforms were called for to deal with voter irregularities. Second, conservative business titan Mike Lindell, whose freedom from addiction story you will read in chapter 7, released the shorter of his two documentaries about the election issues, *Scientific Proof.* (He had released the first, *Absolute Proof,* before our trip.) National media soon began taking those more seriously in the wake of all that had happened.

And finally, while in Florida I received what I felt was an important email from former President Donald Trump's new official press office. It was a simple press release, but I noticed that it had come not to my personal email address but to my email address for *theTHREE.* It was then I remembered that in 2018, I had been vetted by the Trump administration when I had applied for a press pass with them during a Trump event I covered for *theTHREE.* That must have put me on an official press list, on which I apparently still remained, so I decided to take advantage of it and reply to ask for an interview with the Trumps. I told President Trump that his evangelical base was still praying for him and would love to hear from him. I explained that they needed him, and he, them! I received a response from his office saying that my interview request was under review. At the time of this writing (just days after that), that is where it stands.

So have we had that "Oh, thank God" moment yet? Not at the time of this writing. Although many issues and even much corruption have been admitted to and exposed, problems are still being denied in key venues. Getting to the bottom of things will require legal action in a much higher court than has so far been allowed. Perhaps that is the "verdict" I saw when I was watching TV in my "Oh, thank God" dream. All I know it that prophet Kim Clement saw "exposure" and "Spring," just as I had seen "exposure of corruption" and "March 2021," without my ever having known of his 2008 word.

Yet what did the "20–27" numbers mean from my other dream? I was obedient to go on-site and pray during those specific March dates since in my dream the Trumps were standing in the Florida condo I was going to be in during that time. I had also prayed for their rest and *your* rest and reward for your patriotic prayers, large and small. But also it dawned on me while there that upon returning home, we were facing planning the next and probably final eight weeks of episodes in our "America the Beautiful" series for *theTHREE,* which would amazingly be . . . you guessed it . . . episodes 20–27! Time will tell if these shows go on to include an interview with the Trumps, or perhaps news of an "Oh, thank God" proportion.

And that is why I included these two types of dreams in this chapter—so that we might learn how to steward them. So that we might affect the world outside our windows and still be able to experience peace and rest. Prophetic dreams—especially those of a governmental nature—take immense patience and wisdom to push through. No midwife expects to deliver a baby without getting her hands dirty and sacrificing her time, and no prophetic intercessor should expect a neat and easy delivery either. You should not expect to deliver a political dream without getting your knees dirty and sacrificing your time, your heart and even your reputation as you wait and pray with what you "saw." One thing is for sure: The events surrounding the 2020 election and the 2021 White House administration transition have forever changed America. And every prophetic intercessor.

Finally, let me give you another example of how to handle your social media posts, should God seek to use you to help others who are juggling their anxieties about the world outside their window. This is one of my posts from 2016 (also edited for publication here):

> I dreamed in the wee hours today that Donald Trump was praying over me. Now, that was something I never thought I'd see. He was down on one knee, and I myself appeared to be broken on the ground. He had his hands on my head, and his eyes were closed. He was only praying one thing, and it was based on Isaiah 54:17. Trump said, "No weapon formed against your family shall prosper."
>
> I was then awakened (puzzled about what Trump had to do with my family and why God would show me this), and I went back to sleep, dreaming/thinking the rest of the night about posting it as a status update and dreading the reactions. But this dream did not originate with me, and I saw what I saw and couldn't help it.
>
> Yes, I know about the prophecies from a couple of years ago in *Charisma* magazine about how in the 2016 presidential race God would raise up a modern-day Cyrus (Cyrus was named king of Persia in 559 BC and overthrew Babylon in 539 BC). Cyrus was a pagan, non-Israelite king whom interestingly enough, God called His "anointed." He was really good to God's people and helped rebuild

Jerusalem, even financing the project, but also kept building pagan temples on the side. I am sure people in Israel were grumbling and saying, "I do not want this Cyrus guy to have anything to do with rebuilding God's temple. I do not want his blood money. He's a pagan who's playing all nicey-nice with God's people, but I see through it." And it was all true. And yet God called him His anointed. Interestingly, the recent prophecy about God raising up this modern-day Cyrus goes on to say, "But you must understand that he is a bull in a china closet," which I think that we all would agree describes Trump.

What "family" was Trump praying about for me with his head bowed, contrite expression, closed eyes and sincerely concerned tone? Campsmith? That no weapon formed against me and my kids or grandkids would prosper? Or was it the family of God, and that he sincerely wanted no weapon against Christians to prosper? I think it was the latter, and Trump has definitely been a champion of the Church.

I then closed the post with this, and you might consider this type of ending, should God ever nudge you to release a prophetic political dream on social media:

I do not have time to answer comments or private messages on this or even censor them for inappropriate responses that are connected to pro-Trump or anti-Trump, so please do not even respond at all (nor with emails, texts, letters, phone calls, conversations or carrier pigeons). Just read this and pray. If you must, then "react" with one of the Facebook emoticons of like, love, wow, sad, angry, whatever, but just save your words, okay? (Obviously, sharing this on your own page is your prerogative.)

I am happy to say that of the more than one hundred comments and reactions to that post, not a single one was negative. I did go back and remove all the comments, merely because I wanted the focus to be on the dream itself and not everyone's pro-Trump interpretation of it. I do now believe I was right in my hunch that in the dream, I represented the family of God, and that God was showing me Donald Trump's heart not to let any weapon formed against the Church prosper. Has he done it perfectly? That is for God to decide, but between President Trump's love for Israel and his creation of executive orders to protect the religious liberties of Christians, I believe God has used him. I also believe that President Trump knows it.

Television—The Smallest Window in Your Bedroom

We have talked a lot about finding and fielding political prophetic dreams on social media—especially when you are in bed—but now let's talk about that box in your bedroom, the TV. Each time you gaze into it, it is another window that takes you out of your home and into the world. This can be good, but it can also be bad, especially if you are easily influenced emotionally by the news.

A prime example is that I have distinct memories of watching the Watergate hearings on television when I was in third grade. It was 1973, and I was seven years old. It influenced me so greatly that when I heard my school was having a 4-H poetry contest, something in me felt entirely qualified to write a poem about Watergate. Here is what I can remember of it (and please humor me and imagine a little girl reading it to you):

> One thing went on in the courtroom
> for several, several days.
> It was really quite boring
> in the same old way

Then one day as the judge came in
and stood by his desk
he said in a deep, deep voice
"Who's going to protest *no* next?"

The courtroom, it was silent
and then there was a cry
The Secretary said, "I will sir . . .
me myself and I"

She stood up from her desk,
pushed in her chair
looked at her paper
and then just stood there. She said:

Watergate is another word for crime
just think if someone mugs you
or [blah blah blah blah blah blah blah]
It absolutely bugs you!

© Laura Harris, 1973

And that is all I can remember! In the months and months of monotonous hearings, I had heard something about phones being "bugged," and thus, I delivered that last genius line. I laugh just reading it! I did go on to win third place in the contest. Knowing me, I was totally dissatisfied with that, but of course now I realize how peculiarly ambitious it was for a seven year old to tackle politics, not to mention poetry. I just think it is interesting that the evening news made me feel like such an expert that I was willing to stick my neck out and become a political pundit.

Yet aren't we all still doing the same thing today? It is risky, and I hope my guidance and examples here will help show you how to steward your dreams and revelations, should God call you to share them online—or in my line of work, even on television.

Perhaps in another book on another day, I will get to explain why I think this trendy term we are tossing around, the *fake news*, is possibly connected to the prophesied False Prophet, or is even the False Prophet himself. As a media person I certainly hope I am wrong, but I do see it playing out just as Scripture predicts, and I sense it is heading in that direction.

I would like to close this chapter on a happy note, however, with another poem I wrote that urges people to utilize the power of prophetic prayer and declaration in place of worrying about our world. You can go to my YouTube channel to see this poem read aloud and performed during a February 19, 2020, Eastgate sermon that bears the same title as the poem (visit https://youtu.be/c0nm7FAa12U). In that video presentation, you will find compelling images to remind you that this poem speaks not of flesh and blood that we are battling or seeking to dethrone, but of dark spiritual forces and principalities.

Drain the Skies

A campaign promise once was made with circumstance
    and pomp
People shouted and bumpers touted proudly: "DRAIN
    THE SWAMP!"

But nothing's getting drained and at the risk of sounding
    smug
I've come to the conclusion that this swamp just has no
    plug!

The swamp cannot be drained, you see, because it isn't
    there
The conflict you're referring to is happening in the air

We wrestle not with flesh and blood or creatures in a
    swamp
We wrestle against rulers in the sky that strut and stomp

They think that they own cities. They each think they are
    God
So with His warring angels they will always be at odds

Invisible, they hover in the skies o'er land and sea
They want to rule but they cannot, except through you or
    me

And when you feel divisive they have whispered in your ear
They cannot get their schemes fulfilled except through us
    down here

These rulers aren't elected; they are tenured without terms
But they affect elections and get Justices confirmed

And this is why no real change comes despite who comes
    and goes
And why swamps won't get drained until these spirits are
    deposed

We must demand a recount; put demons on the run
And fight THEM, not each other, then impeach them one
    by one

Impeachment or assassination, either one will do.
I am fed up with these city-stealing spirits, aren't you?

But if you're not convinced that there are forces in the
    skies
You need to look no further than into their victim's eyes

We call it Demagoguing; it's political debate
Democracy in action . . . oh but not when parties hate

We must get back to center; the left and right both sin
There's got to be a way that God can help us start again

It starts right at the top though, where honor is reborn
Where faces wear respect and are no longer so forlorn

Where parties cease to sabotage, destroy and misconstrue
And when a leader says they pray there is no doubt they do

Our prayers for them will change things and with Heaven
    looking down
Your prayer becomes the swing vote that will reconcile this
    town

The pow'rs of darkness fear you and they hear your every
    prayer
They know the time has come when they no longer rule
    the air

They'll feel a new wind blowing and a parting of the clouds
Because you paused to think of them and pray this prayer
    out loud:

O God, please heal my country. And let it start with me.
Then please send us revival that's from sea to shining sea

May Washington, D.C., become the place Your spirit dwells
Completely free of fractions, demons, spirits and their
    spells

Bureaucrats be silent! Hear the voice of God!
Repent for your injustice, your division and your fraud

Be baptized in His Spirit and be overcome with love
Create your legislations with God's wisdom from above

And then as all this trickles down to me and you and you
Remember it was all of us that prayed and pushed it through

Then tell your children's children as you look into their
    eyes
It's not that we have drained a swamp but that . . . we've
    drained . . . the skies.

© Laura Harris Smith, February 9, 2020

Again, answer the following questions and save them for when you finish the book. At that time, use today's answers for Day 5 of my "10 Days to a Lifetime of Deeper Sleep and Dreams" program at the close of chapter 10. At the end of that day, a link will be provided that guides you to a good-night video where I pray a blessing over your sleep and dreams.

QUESTIONS AND PRAYER

1. List two current events on the world scene that are trying to rob your peace:

2. List two ways you can begin to share on social media the prophetic dreams God gives you about world events, encouraging others to be at peace:

Pray this out loud: *Jesus, oh how we need to better know You as the Prince of Peace. Please speak to me about what's going on in the world outside my window. Let it enter my bedroom only for the sake of prayer, but never result in panic or stress. Show me how to discipline my use of social media in the bedroom and to think of it as a ministry tool to lead others to You and away from their fears. Through prophetic dreams and discerning prayer, thank You for showing me how to pray for the world, but I also thank You for reminding me that You are in charge of it and not me! In Jesus' name, Amen!*

THE VOICES IN YOUR HEAD

Why is it that you climb into bed each night and every conversation you had that day flashes before your eyes? Like an all-star cast, all the players from that day's soap opera take the stage one by one, under a glaring spotlight.

Unless, that is, you are like my husband and fall asleep in thirty seconds. Then there is no show. It takes me about five minutes to fall asleep, during which I rehash today *and* rehearse tomorrow.

Let's talk about the voices that speak the loudest to you each night as you are trying to sleep: your voice, the skeptics' voices and God's voice.

Your Voice—Ending the Tossing and Turning

According to BuzzFeed, these are the top fifteen questions that you ask yourself at 3:00 a.m. and then wind up googling:

1. What's the difference between regular mint and peppermint?
2. What's the difference between butter and margarine?
3. Can an ice bath help you lose weight?
4. Who invented carrot cake?
5. Do deaf people have an inner voice?
6. If I buy a truck online, does it ship in an even bigger truck?
7. Do helicopters have horns?
8. Can you eat the wrapping paper gum comes in?
9. Who opens the door for the bus driver to get on?
10. Is there such a thing as foot implants?
11. How was popcorn discovered?
12. What is the secret formula for the krabby patty?
13. Is it bad luck to kill a cricket?
14. Do ants fart?
15. Why does shampoo open on the top and conditioner on the bottom?[1]

I promise I did not make those up. Maybe you will confess to asking yourself a couple of them. I came close on numbers 5 and 11. But I do not believe those are really the typical questions you ask yourself in the middle of the night as you are trying to fall asleep. I believe they sound more like this:

1. Is he or she mad at me?
2. Why did I say that today?
3. Why didn't I say this instead?

4. Will I meet my deadline?

5. Is there a fast way to lose weight?

6. What's wrong with me, that I'm not succeeding?

7. How can I make some extra money?

8. Will this person ever change?

9. How can I get ahead in life?

10. Is it too late to call them?

11. Will I wake them up if I text them?

12. How will it go tomorrow?

13. Why didn't they call me?

14. Is God ever going to answer my prayer?

15. Why did I drink that cup of coffee after dinner?!

Sound more accurate? I thought so. And the real dilemma is that you cannot google any of those questions. It is up to you to answer them, and sometimes you have to just give them to God and go to bed, with them yet unanswered. If you do not, you will just lie there and toss and turn.

I am not going to mince words with you. The only way you can silence the inner critic and cynic is to be transformed by the renewing of your mind. And the best way to do that is with God's Word. Why? The answer is in Hebrews 4:12: "For the word of God is living and active, sharper than any two-edged sword, piercing to the division of soul and of spirit, of joints and of marrow, and discerning the thoughts and intentions of the heart."

The Bible is not just ink and onionskin paper. The words inside are actually alive and have the power to re-create and reshape your entire world. We know this because they are God's words, and it was His words that created and shaped our entire world. He did not create the world we live in with a magic wand, with an inner thought or by letting His angels do the grunt work. No, Scripture actually says in its very first chapter, "And God said, 'Let there be light,' and there was light" (Genesis 1:3). He created everything with His words: the sun, the moon, the stars, the oceans, the land, the vegetation, the animals and even humankind. So in our lifelong quest to be more like God, the starting place—the building blocks and the "101" for us—is to speak things into existence the way He did, put faith to our words the way He did, and put His very Word in our mouths. Namely, the Scriptures.

In order to identify the voices in your head as you lie in the dark each night, you need to hold them up in comparison to what God says about you and your situation, so that you can silence everything else. As I said before, the best way to do that is to be transformed by the renewing of your mind. We see this in Romans 12:2: "Do not be conformed to this world, but be transformed by the renewal of your mind, that by testing you may discern what is the will of God, what is good and acceptable and perfect." So this chapter will be full of Scripture to help you weed through the voices in your thinking and only listen to what is true.

The next time you are lying in bed and wondering how popcorn was discovered or how you could lose that extra weight, you need to fill your mind with something else. First of all, if you lie there thinking about the discovery of popcorn long enough, you will have to get up and make some and you will never lose that extra weight! Feed on the Word of God instead. Here are the top Bible verses I have gathered over the years that have a 100 percent success rate in renewing our minds and helping us form new thoughts and patterns. Keep these dozen verses by your bed for nighttime and in your phone for daytime, and begin to commit them to memory. Let them be the answers for any question asked by any voice in your head at night, and you will be on your way to a good night's rest.

> Therefore, prepare your minds for action, keep sober in spirit, set your hope completely on the grace to be brought to you at the revelation of Jesus Christ.
>
> 1 Peter 1:13 NASB

> We are destroying arguments and all arrogance raised against the knowledge of God, and we are taking every thought captive to the obedience of Christ.
>
> 2 Corinthians 10:5 NASB

> Set your minds on the things that are above, not on the things that are on earth.
>
> Colossians 3:2 NASB

> Trust in the LORD with all your heart and lean not on your own understanding; in all your ways submit to him, and he will make your paths straight.
>
> Proverbs 3:5–6 NIV

> Cast your cares on the LORD and he will sustain you; he will never let the righteous be shaken.
>
> Psalm 55:22 NIV

> Peace is what I leave with you; it is my own peace that I give you. I do not give it as the world does. Do not be worried and upset; do not be afraid.
>
> John 14:27 GNT

For God has not given us a spirit of fear, but of power and of love and of a sound mind.

2 Timothy 1:7 NKJV

When anxiety was great within me, your consolation brought me joy.

Psalm 94:19 NIV

But now, this is what the Lord says . . . : "Do not fear, for I have redeemed you; I have summoned you by name; you are mine."

Isaiah 43:1 NIV

Anxiety weighs down the heart, but a kind word cheers it up.

Proverbs 12:25 NIV

I can do all things through him who strengthens me.

Philippians 4:13

So we do not lose heart. Though our outer self is wasting away, our inner self is being renewed day by day.

2 Corinthians 4:16

The Skeptics' Voices—Silencing the Naysayers

Why do we doubt ourselves? We have every reason to expect that we will succeed and thrive, unless someone, somewhere, has told us otherwise. Then the seed is planted: *Will I make it? Will they choose me? Will I be happy? What if they reject me?* You try to get these questions out of your head, but they inevitably haunt you, especially when you are lying in the dark and trying to find peaceful sleep.

It is imperative that you become convinced for yourself of who God says you are, so that no other voices can change your mind. And these skeptical voices come from the oddest of places, when you are least expecting it. Perhaps it is a dressing-room clerk who looks at you with judgment because you need a larger size. You go home, and all you can think about is that you must be fat and unworthy of looking your best. Sure, if you have weight issues you need to address them for the sake of your health, but you have the right to dress with excellence and look your best while on your journey.

Or maybe it is a neighbor who does not agree with how you are raising your children. You always feel he or she is talking about you behind your back, and you can feel the stares when just walking from your car to your front door. I am blessed with good neighbors who have been on either side of me for more than 25 years. Yet during that time, I have seen a lot of young families come into the neighborhood and go, and I know they probably did not agree with all our parental methods. I decided to homeschool all six of my children, and our house was a bustling, loud place. My children were respectful and courteous, but they were creative performing artists who were always filming something crazy—either from the roof, or hanging out of the car or running through the trees. If they were not filming something, they were singing about it, dancing to it, writing about it or taking pictures of it.

But what do you do if the glaring faces and discouraging voices you see and hear in your head at night are not some random store clerk or neighbor? What if the discouraging words came straight out of the mouth of a sister, a brother, a spouse, a child, a teacher, a pastor or a hero? Those voices are a little bit more difficult to drown out. You actually needed the opposite from those people— words of encouragement and affirmation, especially if you were struggling—but all you got was discouragement and rejection. If nobody else has said this to you yet, then I am going to say it here:

I am so sorry.

That may be the only apology you ever get from anyone, so savor it. But I mean it with all my heart. In fact, if I could jump out of the pages of this book or off the screen on which you are reading these words and give you a hug, I would do it! You deserved better and should have at least—at the very, very least—gotten a hug and congratulations for what you have overcome.

People often comment on how confident and unshakable I am when I am on a mission or am facing an impossible task. Let me tell you, I did not get that way from reading a book on self-esteem. I got that way after sitting with God and letting Him affirm me when others rejected me and failed to notice my early accomplishments. The next time you are rejected, replace the hurt in your heart with pity for those people who were never affirmed themselves and therefore have no idea how to affirm you. They are skeptical of the possibility of your success, because they are actually skeptical of themselves.

I have noticed the truth of this for decades now. The very people who discouraged me in my twenties and thirties—who

The next time you are rejected, replace the hurt in your heart with pity for those people who were never affirmed themselves and therefore have no idea how to affirm you.

could not even seem to muster a smile and a "good for you"—
are still unhappy today, decades later. Their lives are sad and
unaccomplished. So the next time one of these people disap-
points you with his or her lack of approval, decide that you are
incapable of disappointment because you have an *appointment*
with God. Sit with Him and allow Him to show you how proud
of you He is. He will even give you good feedback and ideas for
growth and improvement, but it will never be with cynicism or
condemnation.

My head is so full of affirmations from my heavenly Father that
I truly am not hindered or bothered by the naysayers in my life. In
fact, because they have learned this about me, they really have all
disappeared into the shadows. Nobody tries to discourage Laura
Harris Smith anymore. It. Simply. Does. Not. Work.

Yes, I am married to a wonderful man who supports me in
everything I do, but he tends to be quiet. When asked for feedback
(and let me just add that most women do not want to have to
ask for feedback!), he usually says something sweet like, "It was
so good!" And I also have a gaggle of encouraging children, but
when children are young they are still developing their emotional
IQ. Then once they are adults, they are busy using it in their own
households! And the truth is, because I am an encourager myself and because I know the lengths that I go to, to sacrifice for
people so they stay encouraged, I sometimes think I set myself up
for disappointment because of the expectations I have for what
encouragement looks like.

But I will never be a skeptic in someone's life. I will be a cheerleader. I am a realist, and I will tell you the truth and submit
constructive criticism when the time is right. But once I am your
friend, you are stuck with me for life, and I will be your biggest
encourager. You can even choose to walk away and you can even

hurt me, but I will still find something good to say about you behind your back.

I want to be your biggest cheerleader, too. I want to help you drown out the voices of the skeptics in your life, and I especially do not want you to have them screaming at you when you are trying to lie down in peace, hear God and rest. In fact, if it ever gets this bad, you can know for sure that not only have these people in your life not been encouraging; they may have actually been used by the devil himself to try to prevent you from stepping into your future. If such people reject you repeatedly and even leave you, then praise God because He has done you a big favor.

I am a loyal friend. I hate to see a relationship severed, and I never initiate that. But I am now old enough to see that whenever this has happened to us—usually by someone we have met through our ministry who is leaving the church in an unloving way—the Lord has actually done us and the church a huge favor through such people's removal. Notice that I did not say departure. It is often the Lord who has moved these people on for *our* good and for the church's protection.

Try to look at the departures in your life in the same way, and focus your energies on surrounding yourself with more positive encouragers. Especially clear extra time to sit with the Lord and learn what He Himself thinks about you.

I am going to give you an example of how you must sometimes seek God's help in silencing the naysayers, and I want to get detailed and speak to you for just a minute if you are a woman. Recent analytics show that 78 percent of my social media followers and almost 90 percent of my online customers are women. So let me take just a moment to encourage you with something if you are female. (If you are a man reading this, I am about to give you something, too—insight into how you can encourage the women in your life, especially those who have a heart to serve God and who stand on the precipice of spiritual promotion.)

In 2001, the senior pastor and elders approached me at my previous church and invited me to be ordained into ministry. My sixth child was still in diapers and I was homeschooling five kids, but these leaders saw something in me that they said needed recognizing. By just accepting the vow of praying for America, which I told you came about in that dream/cave encounter with the prophet Elisha, the doors had started opening for me to lead others to do the same. After reading Cindy Jacobs's book *Possessing the Gates of the Enemy* (Chosen, 1994) in the late 1990s, I was a new student to the topic of intercession and was determined to throw myself into the world of prayer, reasoning that it was something I could do at home with all of these children.

Then one day, I decided to pick up the phone and contact Generals of Intercession (Cindy and Mike Jacobs's prayer network, now Generals International). I had learned about their United States Strategic Prayer Network, the USSPN (which at the time was the United States Spiritual Warfare Network, the USSWN), and wanted some further information. I merely wanted to know who the Tennessee state coordinator was and where I could sign up to attend prayer meetings to pray for our local government and for America. To my surprise, I got a return fax (yes, that is how long ago this was) offering me the job of state coordinator since there was no one yet in that position for Tennessee!

I literally did not think I could do it and felt totally unqualified. But I learned something about myself during that time. I have the ability to rally people and bring them together. And if you will do that, you will attract the very people to those gatherings who will fill in your gaps and who possess the talents and anointings that you need to get the job done. The next thing I knew, I was packing up the baby (I was always nursing a baby, it seemed) and jumping on a plane to attend meetings with Cindy Jacobs and all the rest of the state coordinators. I usually took along my high school–aged daughter, Jessica, who was an amazing helper with baby Jenesis, but also was a discerning intercessor herself.

Before long, the leaders at the church came and told me that they wanted to ordain me, mainly to affirm what they saw God already doing in my life. My husband was thrilled for me, and my church friends cheered me on, but outside that circle there was either criticism . . . or crickets. We had only been in this charismatic church for about eight years, and we still had friends from the conservative denominational circles we had once moved in. None of those people thought my ordination was biblical. No one said it to my face, but the invitations to have lunch quit coming. So did the calls for speaking engagements on conference circuits where I was regularly invited to speak.

A certain large, conservative Christian bookstore chain even stopped selling a book I had written previously—all because I was now an ordained woman minister. I was still the same woman and the same author with the same writing style, except now I was a heretic. Interestingly enough, years later that chain closed down, and to this day my husband says it is because they would not carry my books (which I doubt, but I humor the thought).

Just as I was about to turn down the invitation for ordination, my husband wrote a letter to my extended family outlining what Scripture says about the topic and asking them to pray for me and to please attend the ordination, which I am happy to say they all did. And my precious father—who himself was the son of a Baptist preacher—said to me, "Baby, all I ask is that you never say *my sermon*. Always remember that it is the Lord's sermon, and if it is not, then you should not be preaching it."

That is why to this day, I never say a teaching is *my sermon*. I have slipped a time or two, but I always try to keep this promise to my father. I also remember when I preached one of my very first sermons and he drove ten hours to hear me. I will never forget the way he navigated through what was new territory for him, always with encouragement and support for me, and you can know that every book I write will always have his name on the cover—Harris—because I am proud to be his daughter.

Still, my father was a minority in my life when it came to people responding to a female ordained minister. Maybe as a woman you are in ministry—or want to be—and you have no encouragers around you and don't even know where to start. You have three choices: (1) You can give up in fear and never walk into your destiny. (2) You can become a man-hating feminist and kick down every closed door, making enemies along the way. Or (3) You can find out what God's Word says about you as a woman in His army, walk confidently toward leadership and climb the ranks.

I would like to give you just a few examples from Scripture of women in influential ministry:

- Deborah judged (see Judges 4:4).
- Huldah prophesied (see 2 Kings 22:14).
- Phoebe was a deaconess (see Romans 16:1).
- Miriam's prophecies directed Israel (see Exodus 15:21).
- Priscilla pastored with husband, Aquila (see 1 Corinthians 16:19).
- Esther guided a kingdom and saved a nation (see the book of Esther).
- God put the Savior of the world in a woman's womb, Mary (see Matthew 1:23).

- Joel and Peter said our sons *and* daughters will prophesy (see Acts 2:17).
- Paul instructed women what to wear in church *when* prophesying—not *if* (see 1 Corinthians 11:5).
- The Gospel was first preached through women running from the empty tomb (see Matthew 28:1–8).
- Tryphena, Tryphosa and Persis were women who "worked hard in the Lord" (see Romans 16:12).

I approach criticism a bit backward, I guess. I try to prove the criticism right and consider what is being said, and then I see if it lines up with God's Word or has any truth in it. In other words, when I am trying to prove one of my points from Scripture for a sermon or in a conversation, I do not get online and look up all the Scriptures to support my blossoming viewpoint. I actually get inside the head of the skeptic and try to disprove what I consider true. I guess you could say it is the opposite of apologetics. If, after doing all of that, I come to the conclusion that I was right to believe as I did, then I will never waver or be able to be convinced otherwise. That is what I did with the topic of women in ministry, and it was only after I had done so that I felt sure God was the one offering me the opportunity.

Let's take my approach with just a few of the voices I heard in my head from the skeptics when I was getting started in ministry. One voice I heard said, *But what about 1 Timothy 2:12, "I do not permit a woman to teach or to exercise authority over a man; rather, she is to remain quiet"?* We women must reckon with this and obey, so let's look at the origins of both "to teach" and "be silent." The Greek for *teach* here is *didasko* and means "to deliver didactic discourses."[2] *Didactic* means "to instruct excessively or teach to an excessive degree." *Didasko* is a prolonged form of the verb *dao* and indicates a perpetual, continual action (that of teaching). So Paul was not saying a woman cannot teach men at all; he was saying she cannot teach them excessively or continuously, which would then support his additional phrase of "or to exercise authority over a man."

As for "be silent," it is the Greek *hesuchia* and means to "be one who does not officiously meddle."[3] It comes from the root *hesuchios*, which means "tranquil, peaceable." Thus, this entire passage is a command for women to be peaceable individuals who do not try to highjack church services, be meddlers or appoint themselves as authority figures in the lives of men.

Another question in my head was, *What about 1 Corinthians 14:34 [NIV], "Women should remain silent in the churches. They are not allowed to speak"?* As for remaining silent, Paul had just told the Corinthian women in chapter 11 what to wear when prophesying in a church service, so for him to demand utter silence three chapters later would be contradictory. As for talking to women about having their heads covered, Corinthian prostitutes were the only unveiled women in society, so Paul did not want the early Church women having to deal with accusations of insubordination (or worse) as they began to exercise their voices when they came together. But this passage undeniably *does* say that women are not to speak, so what do we do with that today? We obey it! *But* we go to the Greek, the language in which the mandate was given, to see how to obey it in full. "To speak" is the Greek word *lalein* and translates as "to speak imprudently, chatter, babble, tweet or make inarticulate sound."[4] Paul was not saying for women never to *speak* at all in church, but never to speak imprudently or inarticulately, and not to babble or chatter during a service. Shouldn't that be said of all of us, male or female?

Furthermore, in 1 Corinthians 14:33–35, Paul goes on to say that if a woman has questions during the church service, she should ask her husband at home. If we are going to interpret that literally and consistently, women should not only be barred from teaching and having authority at church, but they should also be barred from asking questions while at church. Do you know of any church that would turn away a woman with spiritual questions and send her home to ask her husband? What about single women? Are they just out of luck? Will they never learn and grow? It is obvious that we must consider something else in the context of this verse that would help us better apply these instructions today. Remember that in 1 Corinthians 11, Paul had just said that when a woman prays or prophesies in church, she should have a covering on her head. Obviously, for a woman to pray or prophesy in church, she would most certainly have to be speaking. So apparently, Paul felt it was not only permissible, but profitable for women to pray and prophesy aloud in church, as long as they had a head covering (which some denominations take literally to mean a hat, and other individuals like myself believe means a husband or other spiritual head covering).

With all of that dissected, what does it then mean a few chapters later, when Paul says it is disgraceful for women to speak in church? If we let Scripture interpret Scripture, we see from the context of Paul's own letter in its original Greek that, as I previously stated, women are never to *lalein*—to babble, chatter or speak imprudently while at church. God is very serious about this, and I have noticed in my decades in church that women do have the greater propensity toward idle talk. May we as women take seriously this passage to guard our mouths while in the house of the Lord, and especially when using our voices in a church service. May the same be said of our brothers.

My books are read all over the world in places where women are queens, prime ministers and more, and I certainly do not wish to offend you with this next statement if your senior pastor is a woman, or if you are. But I do want to say that as an ordained woman minister who prophesies, I feel most obedient to Scripture when serving in submission to my husband. For years, I was only in the Eastgate pulpit three or four times annually. Then about two years ago, our pastoral team requested that I begin participating in the regular rotation, so now I am in the pulpit monthly. This is where we have landed after spending years studying this topic with the totality of Scripture in the Greek and Hebrew, and also contextually.

In the same manner, consider nations who are led by a woman prime minister or queen. You British men must have revelations American men do not, for many would leave our country if a woman were elected president! Or they would continuously be critical. God must be honoring that "God save the Queen" prayer, because Elizabeth is going strong in her nineties and is currently sovereign over the United Kingdom, Canada, Australia, New Zealand, South Africa, Pakistan, Sri Lanka and a total of 32 nations during her 69 years on the throne.

In short, if you are a man and you were led to the Lord by praying the sinner's prayer with a woman, or you were saved after hearing her preach, you will not be denied entrance into heaven. Nor must you give up your diplomas if you ever had a woman teacher in high school or college. You also do not have to turn the channel or feel guilty if you find yourself learning something from Beth Moore, Joyce Meyer or even me. Or from your precious mother or wife!

Perhaps the best argument for women in ministry is that our God is wise and would never be so foolish as to discharge half of

> God's opinion is the one that matters the most about you. When you lay your head on your pillow tonight, why not ask Him what He thinks?

His army. He needs all of us to roll up our sleeves and do the work of the Gospel. Remember Galatians 3:28: "There is neither Jew nor Greek, there is neither slave nor free, there is no male and female, for you are all one in Christ Jesus."

So settle in your mind what God says about you if you are a woman, whether you were called into ministry, into the marketplace or into motherhood. God's opinion is the one that matters the most about you. When you lay your head on your pillow tonight, why not ask Him what He thinks? Who knows what you will hear? Or dream? But I can guarantee that your answer will come.

God's Voice—The Only Voice That Matters

Finally, then, let's talk about the one voice you need to be able to recognize readily—God's. Rain or shine, valley or mountaintop, and through thick and thicker, His voice needs to be what pierces through it all and centers you in your faith. Immediately.

Perhaps you say you have never heard His voice. Perhaps you have in the past, but it has been a long time. Perhaps you heard it just this morning. Whichever describes you, I know we all agree that we want to hear God more. But how do we do that?

You and I must realize that God speaks in many different ways. Through dreams and visions. Through a whisper or an audible encounter. Through the sermons you hear at church and online. Through His prophets. Through anyone He wants, even a donkey.

And through nature, even the weather (He is the Weatherman, after all). But God can also use secular music, movies and anything from billboards to bumper stickers. It is not unlike any other relationship you have in life. You have one friend who likes to send you cards or an encouraging email, another who likes to speak to you directly on the phone, another who likes to send you flowers, and yet another who wants to sit and chat face-to-face. God is all of those friends rolled up into one. All we must do is be open to receive Him when he speaks—however He sees fit each time—and then respond in faith.

Most of the time when people ask me how to hear God, what they are really asking is how to discern the difference between what is just their own thoughts and what is actually God's voice. We have talked about your own voice in your head, which can oftentimes leave you worried. You know what that sounds and even feels like. Then we discussed the voices of your skeptics and even your enemy, the devil, and those voices more often than not leave you insecure and scared. You know the sound of those voices very well, too. So what you must do—almost by process of elimination—is begin to recognize God's voice as the encourager in your life. And when I say God, I actually mean the Father, the Son and the Holy Spirit. They each speak to you. They each encourage. In fact, some of the names of God (particularly of the Holy Spirit) are Comforter, Helper and Wonderful Counselor. And they will never contradict each other, because they have one voice.

The voice of God will also never contradict Scripture. If it is truly God's voice, it will do one of these twelve things:

- guide you into all truth (see John 16:13)
- discipline you (see Hebrews 12:10)

- convict, but not condemn you (see Romans 6)
- bring salvation and healing (see Romans 10:9–10; 2 Timothy 3:15)
- remind you of God's love (see John 13:1)
- exhort you (see Romans 12:1; Jude 1:3)
- grow your faith (see Romans 10:17)
- bring Scriptures to mind (see John 14:26)
- comfort you (see Psalm 23:4; John 14:16)
- warn you (see Acts 21:4, 10–14; Ephesians 6:4)
- edify you (see Ephesians 4:12)
- instruct you in righteousness (see 2 Timothy 3:16)

Although we come to Jesus by faith, we grow in Him one experience at a time, building a relationship. Hebrews 5:14 (NKJV) says the spiritually mature "have their senses exercised to discern both good and evil." And with that maturity to discern good and evil comes the true gift of learning to discern the Lord's voice in all its forms. And we know that He wants you to recognize His voice, because fifteen times in the New Testament you see the following phrase: "Let him who has an ear to hear, hear!" Matthew, Mark, Luke and John all record this attention-getting slogan. It makes my antennas go up every time I hear it! Imagine if you heard God's voice so clearly that you never made another bad decision, you never entered into another bad relationship, you never made another unwise purchase and you never took any more bad advice. You cannot know that voice and not have an internal desire to obey it. And the best news yet is that He knows your voice, too.

This is the real reason that Christianity can never be a religion. It is a relationship. And the minute you turn it into a religion in your life is the moment you lose the intimacy that Christ wants to enjoy with you. He wants to surprise you, amaze you and make you laugh. He even wants to take your breath away.

Here is a list of ten things God would say to you, and they are all found in Scripture. Perhaps He will not speak these exact words to you on any given occasion, but by reading these words you will get a feel for the kind of encourager your God is, and then you will be able to recognize Him when He speaks:

But Jesus looked at them and said, "With man this is impossible, but with God all things are possible."

Matthew 19:26

But he said to me, "My grace is sufficient for you, for my power is made perfect in weakness." Therefore I will boast all the more gladly of my weaknesses, so that the power of Christ may rest upon me.

2 Corinthians 12:9

Have I not commanded you? Be strong and courageous. Do not be frightened, and do not be dismayed, for the LORD your God is with you wherever you go.

Joshua 1:9

And I will ask the Father, and he will give you another Helper, to be with you forever.

John 14:16

A thousand may fall at your side, ten thousand at your right hand, but it will not come near you.

Psalm 91:7

The one who conquers, I will grant him to sit with me on my throne, as I also conquered and sat down with my Father on his throne.

Revelation 3:21

The one who conquers and who keeps my works until the end, to him I will give authority over the nations.

Revelation 2:26

Nevertheless, I am continually with you; you hold my right hand.

Psalm 73:23

No weapon that is fashioned against you shall succeed, and you shall refute every tongue that rises against you in judgment. This is the heritage of the servants of the LORD and their vindication from me, declares the LORD.

Isaiah 54:17

I have said these things to you, that in me you may have peace. In the world you will have tribulation. But take heart; I have overcome the world.

John 16:33

Again, answer the following questions and save them for when you finish the book. At that time, use today's answers for Day 6 of my "10 Days to a Lifetime of Deeper Sleep and Dreams" program at the close of chapter 10. At the end of that day, a link will be provided that guides you to a good-night video where I pray a blessing over your sleep and dreams.

QUESTIONS AND PRAYER

1. Name two thoughts over which you have the nighttime tendency to toss and turn.

2. Name a voice in your head that you need to silence.

Pray this out loud: *God, I want only one voice in my head—Yours. Through Your Holy Spirit You have allowed me the ability to silence the naysayers who doubt my abilities and to cast all my cares upon You. May I turn to Your Word when anxious, and care more what You think of me than what others do. Right now, I pause to forgive those who have hurt, misjudged or limited me. Today, I choose to listen only to Your voice of affirmation. May it be the last voice I hear as I fall asleep each night, and the first voice I hear each morning as we begin a new and adventurous day. Amen!*

THE JUNK UNDER YOUR BED

At present I am propped up on top of my bed with my laptop, which always sits on top of a HARApad (a slim *Heat And Radiation Attenuating* pad that protects my body from EMFs and radiation). When I write for long periods of time, I am either right here on my bed, or I am on my desk exercise bike. In 2019, I peddled 90.1 miles while writing *Get Well Soon: Natural and Supernatural Remedies for Vibrant Health* (Chosen, 2019) on my bike desk. My book editor, Trish, also acquired one after hearing about mine, and she peddled some additional miles while editing the book. Both of us rode our way through those pages, proving that the pre-designed bicycle on the book cover was pure providence.

I have only written part of this manuscript from the desk bike (and you will find out why in chapter 10), so tonight I am here on the bed as I write this chapter, "The Junk under Your Bed." And it just hit me, what junk is under *my* bed? Years ago, I put my bed on risers to make room for storage. (Remember, that was my bedroom tip number 10 for you: "Put your bed on inexpensive plastic risers to create storage space underneath.") So I admit, I do have a lot of items resting underneath me at present, mostly old framed pictures and paintings that I don't want subjected to the elements of heat and cold in the garage. To my husband, it is junk. To me, it is art.

Did you know it is the same with our emotional junk? You have a perfectly good explanation for why you hang on to every fear and grudge you have. It has become an art form. But someone more objective can easily look under your "bed" and call it junk. Let's examine some of the emotions that keep you up at night and prevent a good night's sleep, and worse, even tamper with your dreams, health and destiny. First, we will face our fear.

Fear—Hidden in Plain Sight

The amygdala—a subregion of the brain that used to be known primarily for being a processing center for fear—is now thought to process many more emotions, too. We have this tiny little almond-shaped piece of our brain processing a constant whirlwind of emotions, practically 24/7 thanks to the media we are exposed to, so it is no wonder our brains are maxed out.

You cannot watch the news without experiencing intense emotional whiplash. Story after story hits you of bad situations with bad outcomes involving bad actors. (No offense to all of my actor friends from my theatre years.) Have you ever stopped for just a moment to consider what is going on inside your brain as you sit under the bombardment of bad news—the rapid gunfire of negativity—for even just *one* newscast? I watched the news the other night as a test and took a count. In thirty minutes, I heard about two murders, one child abduction, two scandals with lawsuits, one missing person, one weather/natural disaster, two celebrity divorces and four political rants. And it was like a lineup of breaking the Ten Commandments. . . . There went number 7, number 9 . . . murder . . . oh, number 6, even number 5. And it is all because we all have a hard time keeping number 1—"You shall have no other gods before me" (Exodus 20:3). Just because a well-tailored, beautiful person on a well-designed, beautiful news set is delivering such news to you in a calm, rational voice, *do not think* it is not impacting your brain negatively. It is.

Nobody wants to feel depressed and sad. Nobody wants to live in fear or be bitter. Nobody wants to feel anxious and worried. But they do and they are. Even Christians. The brain is said to be God's crowning glory of humankind. It comprises only 1 to 2 percent of your total body weight, but it controls 100 percent of your body. Your brain is your boss. It is not your Lord, but it is definitely your boss. It has thousands of different types of neurons, compared to other organs that have fewer than ten types. And one neuron can communicate with as many as two hundred thousand other neurons. Your brain triggers all your human behavior—memories, desires, the ability to make sound decisions, joyous laughter, profound sadness or crying sobs—all of these are brain functions. The brain is the most complex structure scientists have ever studied.

And within the human brain is an amazing, invisible creation called *the mind*. The brain and mind live together yet are totally separate. Within our minds are our emotions—specifically our *limbic brain*, which is the emotional center of the brain. What a miracle!

It is within this very miracle that the enemy jealously seeks to take up residence, making it his playground. He wants to convince you that you are not who God says you are, and that God is not who the Bible says He is. In short, the devil wants to deceive you. It does not happen overnight, but once it happens, he will also destroy you.

"The fear of man lays a snare," says Proverbs 29:25. Think of fear as the highway down which the enemy can drive deception straight into your heart and mind. If you entertain fear, you will be susceptible to a constant barrage of misinformation about God, yourself, those you love and your future. Like a highway with constant tollbooths, you will constantly have to stop and pay a price for traveling down the road of fear. But if, when fear comes, you exit that highway by reminding yourself of the truth about who God is, you will be less susceptible to believing the lies. The lies that tell us God will not help us. That He will not remember us. That He has forgotten us. That He does not see our suffering or trials. And we can best remember who God is and what He does by discovering it in His Word.

Let's take a look at some verses that undoubtedly will remind you that with God in your life, you have nothing to fear. Think of each one of these like an exit ramp you can quickly dart off when you feel your mind racing down the highway of fear.

Do not be anxious about anything, but in everything by prayer and supplication with thanksgiving let your requests be made known to God. And the peace of God, which surpasses all understanding, will guard your hearts and your minds in Christ Jesus.

Philippians 4:6–7

Blessed is the man who remains steadfast under trial, for when he has stood the test he will receive the crown of life, which God has promised to those who love him.

James 1:12

When the righteous cry for help, the LORD hears and delivers them out of all their troubles. The LORD is near to the brokenhearted and saves the crushed in spirit.

Psalm 34:17–18

Not only that, but we rejoice in our sufferings, knowing that suffering produces endurance, and endurance produces character, and character produces hope, and hope does not put us to shame, because God's love has been poured into our hearts through the Holy Spirit who has been given to us.

Romans 5:3–5

Count it all joy, my brothers, when you meet trials of various kinds.

James 1:2

For I consider that the sufferings of this present time are not worth comparing with the glory that is to be revealed to us.

Romans 8:18

Beloved, do not be surprised at the fiery trial when it comes upon you to test you, as though something strange were happening to you.

1 Peter 4:12

In this you rejoice, though now for a little while, if necessary, you have been grieved by various trials.

1 Peter 1:6

For he will hide me in his shelter in the day of trouble; he will conceal me under the cover of his tent; he will lift me high upon a rock.

Psalm 27:5

In the cover of your presence you hide them from the plots of men;
you store them in your shelter from the strife of tongues.

Psalm 31:20

You are a hiding place for me; you preserve me from trouble; you
surround me with shouts of deliverance. *Selah*.

Psalm 32:7

You are my hiding place and my shield; I hope in your word.

Psalm 119:114

Did you notice what those last four verses had in common? As
a child of God, you are *hidden*. Hidden in plain sight! So never
frame your fears as art and sleep on them at night. That is just
junk under your bed and leads to insomnia. If you do get to sleep
that way, it just opens the door to nightmares and night terrors.
While you are cleaning out fear, let's also take a look at some of
the other junk under the bed.

Addictions—Old Habits That Die Hard

By now, you have noticed that this entire book is set in your bedroom and that each chapter walks you through the winding down
process toward a good night's sleep, the releasing of your burdens
to God in prayer, and receiving answers to those prayers through
prophetic dreams: "The Monsters in Your Closet." "The Weapons
under Your Pillow." "The Voices in Your Head." And of course,
this chapter, "The Junk under Your Bed." Now that we are on the
bed, let me take this opportunity to urge you to invest in a good
mattress. We have already established that at 75 years of age, you
will have spent 25 years sleeping, so the investment is worth it.

Yet just as important is your pillow. If you are looking for a good one, look no further than a MyPillow®, my absolute favorite pillow of all time. I bought it long before I met its inventor, the company CEO Mike Lindell, which happened in 2018 when I extended him an invitation to be on my show, *theTHREE*. Like you, I saw Mike on television several times a day. Then one evening my husband urged me to try contacting him.

"Chris," I said, "Mike Lindell isn't going to come on my program!" But after Chris told me several times what a nice guy Mike seemed to be, I gave in and began my search. After reaching out to Mike, I would walk by the television anytime I would hear him say, "Hullo, I'm Mike Lindell. . . ."

I would talk back to him, too: "Hi, Mike! Call me!" It was part greeting and part prayer. And then one day, I heard from him. His publicist was writing to work out the details of his appearance. Mike Lindell was going to be on my show! I could hardly believe it. I had learned about his testimony of deliverance from drug addiction, but honestly, at this point I was still just very excited to meet this larger-than-life entrepreneur.

I had no way of knowing the treat that awaited me. Mike was indeed one of the nicest human beings I had ever met, and I know a lot of human beings! Not just because he appeared on a new show with a TV host he had probably never heard of, but also because he blessed our young ministry by covering his own expenses. I know plenty of entrepreneurs who are nice guys, and plenty of entrepreneurs who are nice guys and vibrant Christians, and maybe even a few of those nice guy, vibrant Christian entrepreneurs are on television. But add to all of that the fact that Mike has such a passion to help people rest well, as I do. And he almost killed himself with sleep deprivation, as I once did. Within minutes of meeting Mike, I could honestly say I had never met anyone like him in the whole world who ticked all those boxes. He was—and is—one of a kind.

It is no wonder that the enemy wanted Mike dead and went to such great lengths to try to kill him so many times. People's jaws dropped again and again throughout my live studio audience as he told us his story during what turned out to be his first televised hour-long testimony. (He first appeared on my show twice for thirty minutes each time, for an hour total.) What is even more amazing is the way God gave him the idea for MyPillow in a prophetic dream. He told the story in our interview:

> One night, I actually had a dream. And the dream was actually the logo "MyPillow" before [I had invented] the pillow. I got up and I wrote "MyPillow" all over the house. And my daughter came upstairs—it's actually in one of the commercials where my daughter came upstairs and she was like nine or ten years old—and she looks and there's like everywhere all the different ways you could connect the Y and the P and she says, "What are you doing"?
>
> And I go, "I'm going to invent this pillow. It's going to be called MyPillow."
>
> There were no "My's" back then, so it kind of sounded weird, and she grabbed her glass of water and goes, "Dad, that's really random."
>
> She went back downstairs, and then a few days later I had another dream about the pillow and maybe what it could do. I mean, these dreams were right from God. I look back and know.
>
> But the kids would say to their mother, "What is with this pillow thing?" Because it would go on for days and then weeks, and then they would go, "Oh, it's just a phase; it'll pass."
>
> And then [the MyPillow production facility] was right across the street a few years later.

But Mike revealed to our viewers that he had a "double track" going on in his life. In the midst of all this revelation was also great addiction. The enemy was trying to steal Mike's future as quickly as God was revealing it to him. Mike continued with the interview,

> I was a cocaine addict for a long time—fifteen to twenty years—and it had changed to crack cocaine in the early 2000s. So when I invented [the pillow], people said all the time, "Wait a minute, you invented MyPillow in 2004–2005 and you quit crack and everything in 2009?!"
>
> That was a miracle in and of itself. Every addict out there knows that addiction is hard work. You try to hide it, and it's hard to keep going. And with crack it's really hard. But I was able to do it. I never broke trust with any of my early business relationships. And I *loved* helping people. That's always been my passion, so when people would come up at these shows and the ones that had my pillow would say, "This pillow changed my life," I would like the story of how it changed their life—the amazing testimony. It would be so dear to me, and I knew, *I've got to keep going in this.*
>
> And I knew even back then that God gave me the pillow for a platform of a much bigger thing. I knew this. I would get this in dreams. I would see these things in the future.

Mike describes getting divorced after twenty years of marriage and how it was "lights out" in the spring of 2007. They were losing everything. The lights were literally going out in his house, yet they were making the pillows in his living room. He was writing labels with magic markers and doing all the shipping with his children, and actually stuffing the pillows in the living room. He didn't know how he was going to get out of his troubles, and people were even trying to take his company. He went heavy into crack after that.

Then one night in 2008, when he was all alone, a phone call came in late from someone who saw a small television ad about the pillow on a public access station. Mike said sometimes he would only get about ten calls in an entire week, and he would answer the calls himself. This particular night at about 6:00 p.m., one woman called and said, "I'm not going to buy a pillow, but God told me to pray for you. Something you're doing is going to be so big to the world." Mike went on,

> I was open to that. So, she was praying and this went on for about fifteen minutes, and she said good-bye. I still have her name to this day. Then about an hour later—this had never happened before— another lady calls up and she said, "God told me to call you and pray for you, that what you're doing is very important. This platform. Whatever this pillow is and whatever it's going to lead to, it's really important, and can I pray with you?"

Mike then described how a third call of the same nature came in from another intercessor a few hours later. Yet he admits that the whole time, he was up doing cocaine. Next, at 4:00 a.m. on the very same night, another call came in from a man who said angrily, "I don't believe in God, but I keep having this dream that God wants me to call you and say that what you're doing is important, and so I hope my dream stops now!" Then he slammed the phone down on Mike.

Finally, at 8:00 a.m. the next morning, the phone rang again and Mike answered it by blurting out, "Let me guess . . . you don't want to buy a pillow, but you want to pray for me?"

The woman on the other end said, "How did you know?!"

Mike prayed with that intercessor, too. His testimony is littered with stories like this of the lengths God went to, redirecting his life. Destiny was calling. God was not giving up.

But neither was Satan. One of the most dangerous components of this story—I now know as a health professional—is that Mike would stay up for days on end without sleep. We have already talked about how this can produce catastrophic neurological ramifications, not to mention emotional, hormonal and cardiovascular ones. Mike knew things were not right in his life, and he describes staying up and working harder and harder to try to fix things.

On one occasion when he lived in one of the worst parts of Minneapolis, Mike had been up for two weeks straight when he had some visitors. A few of his drug dealers showed up, demanding that he go to bed. They said, "You're going to bed and we're shutting you off from everybody, and you're not getting any drugs."

Mike did not even know that these dealers knew each other, yet there they all were, standing in agreement and saying, "You made us a promise. You told us that someday you were going to quit and you were going to come back and help us get out of all this addiction."

Mike had always told them that he was going to do that—prophesying about his future even when he was running from it—and here they were, holding him to his promise. Some of them left, and one stayed to guard him. When the drug lord guarding him fell asleep, Mike went out in the middle of the night to get drugs. Sure enough, nobody on the streets would sell to him. He says they would not even accept one hundred dollars for five dollars' worth of crack cocaine. When he came back in, his buddy grabbed a phone and snapped a picture of Mike in his fourteen-day-long drug-induced, sleep-defiant state. He told Mike he would need the picture one day for a book he was going to write. Sure enough, this very picture is currently on the front cover of Mike's new book, *What Are the Odds? From Crack Addict to CEO* (it is a hologram cover that shifts from the crack addict picture to the present-day Mike when turned toward the light, and how prophetically fitting is that?).

Mike knew now that there was a call of God on his life and that MyPillow would be successful, but that it would not be for the sole purpose of just selling pillows. For millions of people around the world it was a pillow, but for Mike it was a platform that would catapult him into larger spheres of Christian—and governmental—influence.

Finally, after Mike had fourteen near-death experiences, his sister called him. She had always told him that God had picked him for something great, but this time she told him that his window was closing and that if he did not make changes, God was going to have to pick somebody else for what He needed done on the earth. "The time is *now*," his sister said.

Then the Lord led one of Mike's "good buddies" to find him. This was a friend Mike had done drugs with back in the 1980s, but the man had since become a Christian. Mike asked him if life without drugs and life with Jesus was boring. His friend helped Mike shift his perspective by reminding him that addiction is such hard work . . . hard to get money, hard to keep the secret, hard to stay safe, hard to stay alive, even. He helped Mike see that drug addicts who find freedom go on to be some of the hardest workers, best entrepreneurs and most successful people in the world, if they can just get their wounds healed.

Mike was convinced—or wanted to be—so one night in early 2009 he told God in a prayer, *Lord, here's the deal. . . . If You remove the desire for the drugs, I'll "do this platform" and I'm all Yours.*

He woke up the next day expecting to feel terrible, but to his astonishment he had no desire at all for the drugs. None. Yes, he had lost everything. The company had been taken and he had no credit to get anything back, but in just one meeting days later, four investors put forth $7,500 each, so he had the $30,000 he needed to get up and running again.

Mike spent the next several years doing home shows during the day and making pillows with his kids at night, just trying to get back everything he had lost after the years of drug use. He was living in his sister's basement as business began to boom, and within forty days he went from five employees to five hundred. But keep one significant detail in mind: Mike Lindell was still not a Christian! He had not tapped into the wisdom available to all of us when we commit our lives to Jesus. By 2012, even though he was still off all drugs, the business was failing again. This time when Mike stopped to pray, it was to receive Jesus.

When Mike was just two days away from losing everything, God gave him another prophetic dream about where the company was supposed to be as a business by the end of that year. It looked impossible, and Mike likened it to Noah being told to build the ark when he had never even seen rain. So Mike and his investors decided to invest in building a warehouse and shooting a commercial. A previous TV commercial had not done very well, but they learned that once they put Mike himself in the commercials, the business exploded.

Now to date, MyPillow has sold over 50 million pillows and has more than 1,500 employees. Mike has definitely gone on to see the platform that God is using this pillow to build for him. It has included working with President Trump to end drug addiction in America, and also helping addicts find freedom through multiple tools, including his app, his book, the Lindell Foundation and even a movie currently being made about his life.

You would think with all this uphill success, Mike would have a haughty, self-made attitude. Or you would think that all the years on drugs would make him hard and rough. But he is the exact opposite of all that. He is humble, gentle and laser-focused on his mission of promoting the Gospel of Jesus Christ. And as I previously stated, he is indeed one of the nicest people I have ever met. I saw it the very first day with him on the set of *theTHREE*. I open each show with a monologue about my guest—usually three to four minutes long—and I have the reputation of being able to do it on the first take (which the live audience is grateful for). But that day with Mike, it took me three tries. As we stood together backstage on my set, waiting for the musical cue from the live band to make our entrances one more time, Mike looked at me and said, "Laura, don't worry about it. It's probably because of me. Spiritual warfare happens to me everywhere I go."

I took a deep breath after that and we knocked out two of my favorite shows I have ever done on *theTHREE* (which you can see at www.theTHREE.tv). Mike gave away MyPillows to the whole audience and I made a good friend, interviewing him on several other episodes since then. I share Mike's story with you because it is the most extreme addiction story I can think of to encourage anyone out there who might be struggling with the same spirit. Addiction *is* a spirit, and an evil one at that. It has many forms, since we all know that you can be addicted to anything—drugs, alcohol, work, food, people, even ministry. I once heard the story of a man who got off drugs, but not with God's help and not by dealing with it spiritually. Months later, he got addicted to . . . wait for it . . . coupon clipping. It was bizarre to see how this spirit of addiction had come back with a new hairdo.

Much of the world is trying to deal with addiction without Christ's help, and it will not work. It will just show up later in life with even more destructive vengeance. Part of the definition of the word *addiction* is "the fact or condition of being addicted to an activity," and some of its synonyms are "habit, problem, devotion to, dedication to, obsession with, infatuation with, passion for, love of, mania for, or enslavement to."[1] Take a moment to think about your life and any addictive behaviors that the Holy Spirit illuminates to you. Pray this simple prayer here, and remember that Mike Lindell merely prayed a simple prayer, too, and was delivered of his addiction:

> *Father, I know You have a hope and a future for me, and I want it. Please take away this addiction so I can step into the future You have planned and discover why You created me, and then serve You all my days. I give You the addiction, and I receive Your deliverance in return. In Jesus' name, Amen.*

Unforgiveness—The Last Train to Torment

Indeed, even the littlest of offenses may have made a way for the enemy to think that he has a lawful right to distress you. Sure, your grudge may be warranted and totally justified, but there comes a point after you have been trespassed against that you can move into wrongdoing yourself. It is at the point where you decide not to truly pardon a person for what he or she has done to you. That opens the entryway to your torment. Jesus cautioned us of this in Matthew 18:34–35 (DARBY):

> And his lord being angry delivered him to the tormentors till he paid all that was owing to him.
>
> Thus also my heavenly Father shall do to you if ye forgive not from your hearts every one his brother.

This is totally shocking to me, that our caring heavenly Father is so firm with us about what will occur when we do not forgive others. But a considerable lot of us do not. One of the saddest biblical realities must be the quantity of saved, Bible-reading, churchgoing, small group–leading Christians who have been turned over to tormentors. I know a few.

In fact, I used to be one of them, until the Lord taught me a hard lesson. I had to wake up one morning when I should have felt excited about attending an event I had spent weeks preparing for. The problem was, I felt awful. I could hardly move from the couch because my head hurt so badly, even affecting my thoughts and vision. I knew that the Lord wanted me at this event because He had helped me prepare for it and had told me to go, so I was confused about why He would allow me to experience such spiritual warfare in my health. Then He told me that it was not spiritual warfare at all. He showed me that I had been turned over to tormentors after not forgiving several people.

I was so shocked—not because of what I had heard, since I already knew the Scripture we just looked at in Matthew 18, but because He was right. Immediately, several faces popped into my mind, and I released them and the hurt they had caused me to God. I had tried to work things out with these people myself and I still really loved them, but that even further underscored my justification of the silent negative opinion I kept in my heart toward them. I felt the Lord directing me to get up, find a pen and paper, and make a "Forgiveness List."

As the wind blew and the birds chirped that spring day, I sat out there and added one name at a time to my Forgiveness List, until to my surprise it numbered 153 people.

I went outside—headache and all—and sat down near my flower garden. As the wind blew and the birds chirped that spring day, I sat out there and added one name at a time to my Forgiveness List, until to my surprise it numbered 153 people. Once the Lord opened my eyes to what was in my heart, the names just kept coming and coming.

Maybe that number shocks you, and maybe it doesn't. If you have been in ministry for any number of years, you will actually know it is quite a small number. People come and people go. They think you are magnificent and you open your heart to them, serve them with all your strength and faith, go without meals for them, give of your resources to them when they are in need, and then they get what they need and often leave. And when they leave you, that means that their children also leave your children, so there is frequently hurt there, too. It accumulates fast.

When I finished with my list, I did some quick math and discovered that 61 percent of the people on it were indeed ministry related, and 17 percent were family members. That left 22 percent to random friends, doctors who had done me more harm than good, and yes, even those customer service representatives who wasted hours of my time, each on top of refusing to refund the money I knew we were due.

All of those things ruin your day, and when tallied together can ruin your life. But I spoke forgiveness over each name on the list out loud, releasing the person from all my expectations for the future and forgiving him or her for all hurts from the past. I even asked God how many other people's lists my name would appear on, and I asked Him to forgive me for hurting those unknown people.

I felt lighter afterward, and by the end of the whole experience—which took about an hour—my headache was gone, my vision was restored and my thoughts were perfectly clear. Then I took my Forgiveness List and burned it, sprinkling the ashes around a little hibiscus tree that my father had given me, but that would never bloom.

You guessed it—before spring was over, that tree put forth more purple blooms that I could count. The tree was more purple than green, it seemed! And I know why. All my hurt and pain had been the perfect fertilizer for growth when I got rid of it, and I guarantee you that it will be the same for you, my friend. I challenge you to make your own forgiveness list at the end of this chapter, and my prediction is that you will experience both healing and freedom from the effort. You will definitely feel a spirit of torment leave you that may have been afflicting you with sadness, depression, anger, fear, or even just a lack of creative flow or productivity.

One of my favorite books in my doctoral program as a student of naturopathy is Carey A. Reams's book *Choose! Life or Death*. In one section, he speaks extensively about the dangers of unforgiveness and explains that God's Word is the key to total deliverance from such enemies of our faith. He says of the Bible:

> It taught me how to forgive and forget.
>
> It taught me that absolute forgiveness is absolute forgetfulness.
>
> It showed me where I came from, why I am here, and where I am going . . . if I serve Him, if I faint not, if I make restitution for the mistakes that I make, if I ask forgiveness, and if I forgive.
>
> It has made me fearless. I fear not what men can do to me, but I do have one fear. My greatest fear is that I will do something that the Holy Spirit will be removed from me![2]

If you still remain unconvinced that you need to forgive because unforgiveness is the last train to torment, here is my advice to you, straight from Scripture. Don't forgive others if . . .

1. You don't love Jesus.

John 14:24 is clear: "Whoever does not love me does not keep my words."

2. You don't want to be forgiven.

Matthew 6:15 reveals this: "But if you do not forgive others their trespasses, neither will your Father forgive your trespasses."

3. You want your prayers to go unanswered.

Mark 11:24–25 says,

> Therefore I tell you, whatever you ask in prayer, believe that you have received it, and it will be yours. And whenever you stand praying, forgive, if you have anything against anyone, so that your Father also who is in heaven may forgive you your trespasses.

Matthew 7 adds, "Ask, and it will be given to you; seek, and you will find; knock, and it will be opened to you. . . . So whatever you wish that others would do to you, do also to them" (verses 7, 12). In John 15 we see that when we abide in Christ we will have spiritual fruit, and that the way we abide in Jesus is by keeping His commandments (see verses 5, 10). We also see that His commandment is to love one another as He loves us (see verse 12), and that if we abide in Him (by keeping His commandments), and His Word is in us, we can ask anything and it will be given us (see verse 7). The reason a lot of our prayers go unanswered is because we are not observing the commandments given clearly to us; therefore, we are not abiding in Christ's love. If we are not abiding there, how can we think He will hear our prayers?

4. You want to become defiled.

Don't forget Hebrews 12:15: "See to it that no one fails to obtain the grace of God; that no 'root of bitterness' springs up and causes trouble, and by it many become defiled." Notice at the end it says that many are defiled. This root of bitterness is a *very* common—if not one of the most common—everyday thing that defiles people! A person can shed many bondages by forgiving those who have wronged him or her.

5. You want to give Satan an advantage.

Second Corinthians 2:10–11 says, "Anyone whom you forgive, I also forgive. Indeed, what I have forgiven, if I have forgiven anything, has been for your sake in the presence of Christ, so that we would not be outwitted by Satan; for we are not ignorant of his designs."

6. You want to be kept out of heaven.

Matthew 7 shows us in verses 12 and 21,

> So whatever you wish that others would do to you, do also to them, for this is the Law and the Prophets. . . . Not everyone who says to me, "Lord, Lord," will enter the kingdom of heaven, but the one who does the will of my Father who is in heaven.

And remember 1 John 3:14: "We know that we have passed out of death into life, because we love the brothers. Whoever does not love abides in death."

7. You want to bear no spiritual fruit.

John 15:5–12 tells us forthrightly that if we abide in Christ, we will produce much spiritual fruit. Verse 10 tells us that the way we abide in Christ is by keeping His commandments. Verse 12 tells us that His commandment is that we love one another as He has loved us. That is a tall order, but think about it: If we do not love one another as He has loved us, then we do not abide in Him, and how are we supposed to produce any spiritual fruit if we do not abide in Him? According to verse 6, the branch that does not abide in the vine will be cast into the fire.

8. You want to be open to curses.

When God's children in the Old Testament disobeyed His commandments, it opened them up to numerous curses (see Deuteronomy 27:26). Today when we disobey God, we can experience many curses, too. These curses can cause financial difficulties, divorce and infidelity, physical problems, emotional and mental problems, childlessness, and so many more issues (see Deuteronomy 28). What is worse is that a curse can be handed down to your future generations (see Exodus 20:5); these are called generational curses.

9. You want to be tormented demonically.

Consider Matthew 18:23–35 the next time you are faced with deciding between forgiving someone or holding a grudge:

Therefore the kingdom of heaven may be compared to a king who wished to settle accounts with his servants. When he began to settle, one was brought to him who owed him ten thousand talents. And since he could not pay, his master ordered him to be sold, with his wife and children and all that he had, and payment to be made. So the servant fell on his knees, imploring him, "Have patience with me, and I will pay you everything." And out of pity for him, the master of that servant released him and forgave him the debt. But when that same servant went out, he found one of his fellow servants who owed him a hundred denarii, and seizing him, he began to choke him, saying, "Pay what you owe." So his fellow servant fell down and pleaded with him, "Have patience with me, and I will pay you." He refused and went and put him in prison until he should pay the debt. When his fellow servants saw what had taken place, they were greatly distressed, and they went and reported to their master all that had taken place. Then his master summoned him and said to him, "You wicked servant! I forgave you all that debt because you pleaded with me. And should not you have had mercy on your fellow servant, as I had mercy on you?" And in anger his master delivered him to the jailers, until he should pay all his debt. So also my heavenly Father will do to every one of you, if you do not forgive your brother from your heart.

At the point when we forgive, it frees us up to receive God's absolution, it places us in a better position to receive when we pray, it encourages us to become profoundly productive, and we will realize that we have passed from spiritual demise to being reconnected with our great Father when we love one another (see Matthew 6:15; Mark 11:24–25; John 15:5, 10, 12; 1 John 3:14). At the point when we keep God's precepts and love each other, absolving each other of our wrongdoings, we demonstrate that we love Jesus and we live in Christ's love itself (see John 14:21; John 15:10). What a sublime gift absolution truly is!

Forgiveness

It feels like a good rubdown when you've failed and done
   your worst
It seems a noble option, 'til you're asked to give it first

It tastes like milk and honey when it's offered down to you
Yet smells to the high heavens when you did not get your
due

It sounds like angels singing when it's offered and received
Yet when we won't extend it, bitterness is then conceived

It does not search for justice or agree to disagree
It cuts the flesh, reveals the heart, releases destiny

© Laura Harris Smith, August 2000

Again, answer the following questions and save them for when you finish the book. At that time, use today's answers for Day 8 of my "10 Days to a Lifetime of Deeper Sleep and Dreams" program at the close of chapter 10. At the end of that day, a link will be provided that guides you to a good-night video where I pray a blessing over your sleep and dreams.

QUESTIONS AND PRAYER

1. List your two worst fears. Now think about if they came true and imagine how you believe God would rescue you.

2. Name two significant people in your life whom you need to forgive.

Pray this out loud: *Heavenly Father, I have fears that the enemy whispers to me that no one but me hears. Silence him as I make the decision by faith to listen to Your promises and not his lies. Right now, I ask You to deliver me from the addictive tendencies I have that hold me back and prevent me from moving forward in You, or even sleeping well at night. Finally, I fully release to You those people who have maligned and wounded me. Those people I loved and let into a deep space in my heart reserved only for those I trust. I forgive them. I pray they might be healed and wound others no more. In Jesus' name, Amen.*

THE WRITING ON THE WALL

Think of your life as a house, and each area of your life as a room. Work is one room. Church and ministry are another room. Your relationships are another room. Your private thoughts have their own room, too (or at least a closet).

Now imagine that the walls of each room contain messages written by the finger of God to guide you: "the writing on the wall." But you keep buying new paint to cover up the obvious because you do not want to make the changes the messages require.

Have you ever thought about what these messages would be? Let's explore a few—namely, the reasons you don't pray, you don't confront your unbelief and you don't confront your blockage to praying in the Spirit. We will start with prayerlessness first.

Prayerlessness—Confronting Reasons You Don't Pray

According to a Pew Research Center article written in 2014, 55 percent of Americans say they pray every day, 21 percent say they pray weekly or monthly, and 23 percent say they seldom or never pray.[1] Even among those not affiliated religiously with any denomination or particular church, 20 percent say they pray daily. Did you know that 64 percent of women say they pray every day, while only 46 percent of men do? And did you know that Americans 65 and up are far more likely than 30-somethings or even younger to say they pray daily (65 percent versus 41 percent)? Put together, that means the majority of people who truly pray daily are older women. Yep, your praying grandma.

In the late 1990s the Promise Keepers approached me to ask if I would be the prayer coordinator for their event that was coming to Nashville. It was 17,000 men and me there that day. My main job was to pray over every aspect of the event because those men believed in the power of prayer—so much that I would be going back and forth, up and down the stairs of what is now called the Bridgestone Arena, and I would hear on my little radio headset, "Where is Laura Smith? Get her up here to pray because the cash register door is jammed and nobody can fix it! There's a line forming!"

So I would run and pray, back and forth, wherever they needed me. My other job was to assemble a prayer team who could be praying nonstop together and just really saturate that place with the Holy Spirit while I was running back and forth and rebuking cash register demons, I guess. But I noticed that they had put my prayer team down in the belly of the building—the basement, in fact—away from everything. I asked why.

Their answer matched one of the statistics I just cited. They said, "We put you downstairs, near a direct entrance that would not require long walks from a parking lot, because it is our experience that most intercessors are older women who do not walk very well."

I kid you not. But as I thought about it, I realized how true it is. This should not be the case! They got me thinking about why it might be true, and I decided that the secret lies in what we perceive to be inactivity. Maybe these older intercessors are the only ones sitting still! The rest of us are busy running around trying to fix all our own problems. We do not give it to God, because we can do it better than He can—or so we deceive ourselves into believing.

I certainly can attest to the fact that when I have found myself sidelined in life and being forced to rest physically, my faith in prayer has grown to a whole other level. Could it perhaps be because I realize that the answers that come actually have nothing to do with me or my skills, ideas or negotiating prowess? I think there are nuggets of truth in this theory, and we ought not wait until we are older and less active to see our prayer lives mature. From all of this, we see that one of the first ways to confront our prayerlessness is to confront our busyness.

We also need to confront our hope, or lack of it. Some of us no longer pray because we no longer hope. We have switched off hope the way we switch off a lamp. Perhaps you have prayed too long about a situation that you feel God could have answered long ago, but what you do not realize is that the bigger the prayer request, the longer it may take. What if it involves the free will of other people? God does not magically wave a wand and force people to robotically do what you have prayed for. In fact, prayers to override other people's free-will choices would be borderline witchcraft. We must be patient and allow God to do the full work required to get our big prayer requests answered. And while we wait, we need to move from just praying about our problems to seeing ourselves on the other side of their answers. Proverbs 23:7 (KJV) says, "For as he [actually, as anyone] thinketh in his heart, so is he."

Let's dream a little bit. Imagine that you wake up tomorrow and all your prayers are answered. Every. Single. One. Contemplate what that would look like in each of the following twenty areas, and you might even grab pen and paper and jot down those contemplations. What would answered prayers look like . . .

1. in your extended family?
2. in your occupation?
3. in your body?
4. in your character?
5. in your attitude?
6. in your mind?
7. in your goals?
8. in your friendships?
9. in your love life?
10. in your house?
11. in your church?
12. in your neighborhood?
13. in your city?
14. in your country?
15. in your prayer life?
16. in your bank account?
17. in your children?
18. in your travels?
19. in your communication skills?
20. in your relationship with God?

I hope this list inspires you to pray with greater hope. Remember that sometimes we are not waiting on God, but He is waiting on us. What do I mean by that? I actually discussed this in a sermon once and called it the "If-Then" sermon, meaning if we do a certain thing, then God says He will do a certain thing. It could also be called the "If You, Then I Will" sermon (the *if you* being the request God makes for our obedience, and the *I will* being whatever it is that God is promising you once you comply). While nobody likes the idea of God and stipulations, even our salvation comes with one: *believe.*

Here are some *if-then*, or *if you–then I will* Scriptures (all from the NIV, with emphases added). If we do not do the *if*, God will not do the *then* or *I will*, for our own good.

If you are willing and obedient, *you will* eat the good things of the land; but *if you* resist and rebel, *you will* be devoured by the sword.

Isaiah 1:19–20

The LORD *will* make you the head, not the tail. *If you* pay attention to the commands of the LORD.

Deuteronomy 28:13

I am the vine; you are the branches. *If you* remain in me and I in you, *you will* bear much fruit; apart from me you can do nothing.

John 15:5

If you believe, *you will* receive whatever you ask for in prayer.

Matthew 21:22

All these blessings *will come* on you and accompany you *if you* obey the LORD your God.

Deuteronomy 28:2

Therefore, my brothers and sisters, make every effort to confirm your calling and election. For *if you* do these things, *you will* never stumble.

2 Peter 1:10

Now that you know these things, *you will* be blessed *if you* do them.

John 13:17

By this gospel you are saved, *if you* hold firmly to the word I preached to you. Otherwise, you have believed in vain.

1 Corinthians 15:2

For *if you* forgive other people when they sin against you, your heavenly *Father will* also forgive you. But *if you do not* forgive others their sins, your *Father will not* forgive your sins.

Matthew 6:14–15

If you pay attention to these laws and are careful to follow them, *then the* LORD *your God will* keep his covenant of love with you, as he swore to your ancestors.

Deuteronomy 7:12

Finally, the following if-then promise especially applies to this section on confronting our prayerlessness. I pray that it serves as the final motivator you need in order to let prayer begin to interrupt your schedule and busyness more often:

If my people, who are called by my name, *will* humble themselves and pray and seek my face and turn from their wicked ways, *then*

I will hear from heaven, and *I will* forgive their sin and *will heal* their land.

2 Chronicles 7:14

Doubt—Confronting Your Unbelief

CBS has done a study about faith. Are you ready for this? They took a poll and asked Americans a simple question: "Do you believe in miracles?" Nearly four out of five people answered yes, they believe miracles occur. The exact numbers were 78 percent yes and 19 percent no.[2]

The study went on to say that 63 percent of those yes people also say that while they believe in miracles, they have never seen one. Amazing! Seeing is not necessarily believing—not to this group of Americans. They believe, but do not see. I think this is called *faith*! The poll went on to say that of the 78 percent who believe in miracles, 19 percent of them are not even Christians. I think there is something subconscious inside all of us that knows we need supernatural help. The kind of help that defies the laws of nature and all logic. I guess it is true: Blessed are those who do not see, but believe.

More than one-third of America's general population, however—35 percent—say they *have* seen a miracle. And that number jumps to a whopping 59 percent in what the study calls the "extremely religious" group. (What does that even mean, "extremely religious"?!)

Next, 87 percent of Americans think that personal prayer or other spiritual or religious practices can help sick people medically. But far fewer actually believe in "miracle healers," people who have the ability to heal someone with a touch. This secular study was describing the biblical laying on of hands. Surprisingly, only one-third of Americans believe in that. A clear majority, 61 percent, do not even believe in its legitimacy. And do you remember that "extremely religious" group? Believe it or not, they also doubt and tend to reject believing in healers. Decide today never to be in that group. The Pharisees got to walk alongside Jesus Christ Himself, yet they missed Him entirely. Never be a Pharisee! You will miss Jesus every time.

Yet despite that high number for doubters, one-quarter of Americans say that they have been cured of an illness as the result of prayer. I certainly have, many times. (I will tell you one recent story about it in chapter 10.)

> The top reason atheists cite for leaving Christianity is "unanswered prayer."

Let's talk for a moment about what happens when you decree and you believe, yet nothing changes. The top reason atheists cite for leaving Christianity is "unanswered prayer." We must decide what we believe, dig in our heels and never turn back. In my decades of ministry, I have noticed a common pattern with people who fall away from their faith. If you have never heard the word *apostate*, then you need to familiarize yourself with it because it is becoming increasingly easier for a Christian to become one.

The dictionary definition of *apostate* is "a person who renounces a religious or political belief or principle" (noun) and "abandoning religious or political belief or principle" (adjective).[3] So in short, an *apostate* commits *apostasy*, which is defined as "the abandonment or renunciation of a religious or political belief."[4]

You see it happening more and more in these last days. And it is not just an occasional friend or a nameless neighbor, but high-profile Church leaders. It is so sad to watch—not just what happens to an individual who sabotages his or her own platform and ministry to a congregation, but what happens to the faith of those who are watching the person as it unfolds. Jesus was right when He said that if you strike the shepherd, the sheep will scatter (see Matthew 26:31).

One day many years ago, I finally sat down and came up with a list of the ten steps that I notice always lead to apostasy. I call this list "The Anatomy of Apostasy." If you see any of these early signs in your life, then do not leave them unattended. Never let them go unchecked. If you will be brave and confront your doubts early on, paying special attention to your connection to the Body of Christ, you will never become an apostate. Here are the ten stages to look for, which usually occur in this order:

1. *The Trials Phase.* The enemy plants trouble and trial into your life as a believer (in your finances, health, family, etc.).

2. *The Secular Influences Phase.* You begin to consult ungodly friends and secular influences for counsel instead of God's Word (e.g., parenting calmer instead of disciplining your children, seeing a counselor instead of first seeing a pastor, working harder instead of observing the Sabbath, etc.).

3. *The Doubts Phase.* Doubt creeps in about God—doubts about His existence, His love, His desired level of involvement in your day-to-day life.

4. *The Church Deprioritization Phase.* The search for self-improvement begins to replace your desire for a community of believers. You deprioritize Sundays and miss church often.

5. *The Making Excuses Phase.* People at church begin to reach out to you, and you make excuses. You have not entirely lost your belief in the local church, so it still matters to you what these people think. But you no longer cultivate relationships with them as you once did.

6. *The Bridge-Burning, Offended Phase.* Time goes by and you are now out of fellowship with your church family. Those people have shifted their relationships, and you learn of it. Offense enters. And pride, which precedes a fall.

7. *The Secular Surrender Phase.* The loss of Christian fellowship and lack of time in God's Word now leave you feeling a real void. Your peace is gone, but you are too proud to return to the Prince of Peace or to Christian fellowship. Since you are still out of God's Word, your life is devoid of any wise counsel. You now fully pivot toward secular influences to find peace.

8. *The Substitutions Phase.* That pivot causes the greatest compromises of your life. You crave peace but have burned bridges with the Prince of Peace and have cut ties with His family. You therefore now reach for substitutions like yoga or meditation for peace, and you use substances like alcohol or drugs (whether prescription or illegal) for relaxation. Those substitutions open up your spirit to evil, deceiving spirits that crowd out the Holy Spirit and His resulting holiness in your life.

9. *The Deception Phase.* You begin to make the worst decisions of your life. You think they are the best decisions of your life. You are fully deceived and those closest to you now see it, but you have gotten rid of all your true friends and burned those bridges.

10. *Apostasy.* The combination of the original trials, choosing secular over biblical counsel, disfellowshiping your church family, and the pride that caused you to burn bridges to prove what you could do on your own have now caused you to despise what you once considered precious. You now doubt the validity and infallibility of the Bible itself, and eventually you doubt the resurrection of Jesus. *You are exactly where the enemy wanted you when he patiently invested those trials into your life. You are a sheep outside the sheepfold, marked for slaughter and now defenseless.*

What is most sad is that the last phase actually is not a phase. It is final. Apostasy is the death of your faith. That is not to say that you cannot regain your faith, because you can. No matter how far away from God you get, it is only one step back. Yet the one who has chosen the path of apostasy and then returned must truly make changes to prevent falling once again into unbelief. In order to do that, you must confront your unbelief.

It is true that prayers sometimes go unanswered because of sin, apathy, pride, unforgiveness, rebellion or other iniquities. We know this because Psalm 66:18 (NKJV) says, "If I regard iniquity in my heart, the Lord will not hear." But sometimes there is another explanation for why one's prayer life feels lifeless. Sometimes it is because you are doing all the praying instead of allowing the Holy Spirit to pray through you. Let's discuss that next.

Spirit Prayer—Confronting Your Blockage

Next to the blessing of salvation, if I had one additional blessing I could ensure that every Christian had, and if I somehow had the ability to convince them all that they should not stop asking, seeking and knocking until they fully experienced it, it would be this: the baptism of the Holy Spirit, with the evidence of speaking in tongues and the daily use of that as a prayer language.

This Spirit baptism and its subsequent disciplines changed my life drastically after seventeen years of already loving Jesus with every fiber of my being, and even after already being in ministry. In fact, it made me love Him even more. But since the Holy Spirit is a distinct and separate personality of the Trinity, His "fullness" in my life has had a distinct impact on my own personality. I became more creative, more energized, more positive, more daring. (The Holy Spirit is a faith-boosting Mastermind, so expect a shift once He hits the scene!) Yet somehow, despite my sudden ability to take more risks, pray harder and worship louder, I was much calmer. Happier and more content. Less troubled by the woundings of the past and the grievances of the present.

Ask anyone who knew me prior to and just after 1993, when the baptism in the Spirit came. I was different. My kids will tell you. My parents will tell you. My husband will tell you. Or read my writings from around that period, and they will convince you. Still, even though countless Christians hear these types of glowing testimonies about the baptism, they are skeptical. Perhaps they have seen a poor representation of the "charismatic Christian" lifestyle, either in person or on television. Perhaps they do not thoroughly understand where this blessing is in Scripture, so they say, "Jesus is all I need." But since, as I said, I have the desire to make sure every Christian experiences this blessing, and since here you are, sitting here reading one of my books, I am going to ask you to pause with me for a few minutes and let me address what I believe are the twelve most common blockages to receiving the baptism of the Holy Spirit. (If this is not an issue for you and you have had no blockages in this area, stop and think of people you know who do. You may know someone, or several someones, who have a blockage in this vital area of life in the Spirit. Consider recommending that they read this section of the book.)

Here are the top twelve blockages, in no particular order:

1. You're not even sure what the baptism of the Holy Spirit is.

Let's first look at God's Word since you should be forming all of your opinions entirely upon it, and not on someone else's perspective or experience. John the Baptist's words in Matthew 3:11 were, "I baptize you with water for repentance, but he who is coming after me is mightier than I, whose sandals I am not worthy to carry. *He will baptize you with the Holy Spirit and fire*" (emphasis added). We see here that the baptism of the Holy Spirit is not some beady-eyed, wild and unbiblical doctrine. It is what Jesus has planned for you. He desires it for you. Notice in the Bible the three ways that the Holy Spirit operates—the three prepositions that describe His movements whenever He is mentioned in the New Testament:

- *para* (Greek *with*)—This is when the Spirit of God surrounds and then woos a person to Christ before salvation and is then *with* him or her, as used in John 14:17 (NIV): "But you know him, for he lives with you and will be in you."
- *en* (Greek *in*)—When the Holy Spirit comes to live *in* the believer at the point of salvation, as used in John 14:20 (NIV): "On that day you will realize that I am in my Father, and you are in me, and I am in you."

- *epi* (Greek *upon* or *on*)—This is different than the Spirit being with you or in you; this is Him coming *upon* you and baptizing you completely, as used in verses such as these:
  - » Acts 1:8 (NIV): "But you will receive power when the Holy Spirit comes on you; and you will be my witnesses in Jerusalem, and in all Judea and Samaria, and to the ends of the earth."
  - » And Acts 8:16 (NIV): "Because the Holy Spirit had not yet come on any of them; they had simply been baptized into the name of the Lord Jesus."
  - » Also Acts 10:44 (NIV): "While Peter was still speaking these words, the Holy Spirit came on all who heard the message."
  - » And finally, Acts 19:6 (NIV): "When Paul placed his hands on them, the Holy Spirit came on them, and they spoke in tongues and prophesied."

Friend, the Holy Spirit wants so much more than just to be near or in you. He wants to fully immerse you in every good thing He has for you. As I like to say, He wants to fondue you in Himself! The baptism of the Holy Spirit is usually a one-time event that is often accompanied by speaking in tongues (the prayer gift, which we will discuss more in a moment). And afterward, that type of prayer can and should happen again and again. So tongues can accompany the baptism of the Holy Spirit, but can also come before or after it.

2. Your denomination de-emphasizes Holy Spirit baptism, and you can't remember any instances in the Bible of people praying in tongues.

Someone who says this has never read the book of Acts while hungry—I mean, *really* hungry for more of God! Because if you are that hungry, you don't miss it. Look at these verses from the book of Acts:

For John baptized with water, but you will be baptized with the Holy Spirit not many days from now.

Acts 1:5

And they were all filled with the Holy Spirit and began to speak in other tongues as the Spirit gave them utterance.

Acts 2:4

So Ananias departed and entered the house. And laying his hands on him he said, "Brother Saul, the Lord Jesus who appeared to you on the road by which you came has sent me so that you may regain your sight and be filled with the Holy Spirit."

Acts 9:17

While Peter was still saying these things, the Holy Spirit fell on all who heard the word. And the believers from among the circumcised who had come with Peter were amazed, because the gift of the Holy Spirit was poured out even on the Gentiles. For they were hearing them speaking in tongues and extolling God.

Acts 10:44–46

And it happened that while Apollos was at Corinth, Paul passed through the inland country and came to Ephesus. There he found some disciples. And he said to them, "Did you receive the Holy Spirit when you believed?" And they said, "No, we have not even heard that there is a Holy Spirit." And he said, "Into what then were you baptized?" They said, "Into John's baptism." And Paul said, "John baptized with the baptism of repentance, telling the people to believe in the one who was to come after him, that is, Jesus." On hearing this, they were baptized in the name of the Lord Jesus.

Acts 19:1–5

And when Paul had laid his hands on them, the Holy Spirit came on them, and they began speaking in tongues and prophesying.

Acts 19:6

So yes, despite what your denomination has or has not been emphasizing to you, the Word of God itself is calling out to you with an invitation to experience this baptism and its resulting prayer gift.

3. You are uneasy about this topic.

As I said in number 1, speaking in tongues is just the prayer gift. Think of it as perfect prayer. You are allowing the Holy Spirit to pray *through* you. And remember, you can trust God. He would never give you something that is bad for you, as Jesus assured us in Matthew 7:9–11:

Which one of you, if his son asks him for bread, will give him a stone? Or if he asks for a fish, will give him a serpent? If you then, who are evil, know how to give good gifts to your children, how much more will your Father who is in heaven give good things to those who ask Him?

4. You see this baptism now in the book of Acts, but you are not sure if God speaks anywhere else about using this prayer gift, or about its validity.

The apostle Paul outlines this exactly in his first letter to the Corinthians, when he teaches on the nine gifts of the Holy Spirit. Two of those gifts are speaking in tongues and the interpretation of tongues (see 1 Corinthians 12:4–11). And then later, Paul gives instruction on how those gifts are exercised for the good of all, for example in a church service. The entire chapter of 1 Corinthians 14 speaks to both the validity and the necessity of using this gift when in prayer. In verse 14 Paul tells us, "For if I pray in a tongue, my spirit prays but my mind is unfruitful." So praying in tongues is Spirit prayer. It is praying with your spirit and not your mind. It is praying what is on God's mind regarding a matter, and not what is on yours.

5. You think that praying in tongues is for someone else besides you.

"Now I want you all to speak in tongues," says Paul in 1 Corinthians 14:5. God wants you earnestly to desire spiritual gifts. The gift of tongues will build you up, but of course, God's higher goal is to build up the entire Church. Paul explains it further in verses 1–4:

> Pursue love, and earnestly desire the spiritual gifts, especially that you may prophesy. For one who speaks in a tongue speaks not to men but to God; for no one understands him, but he utters mysteries in the Spirit. On the other hand, the one who prophesies speaks to people for their upbuilding and encouragement and consolation. The one who speaks in a tongue builds up himself, but the one who prophesies builds up the church.

6. You are confused about whether or not "praying in the Spirit" is the same as "tongues."

I am happy to tell you that yes, they are the same act. Paul says, "For if I pray in a tongue, my spirit prays" (1 Corinthians 14:14). So you may use "praying in the Spirit" interchangeably with "praying in tongues."

7. Ministry-wise, you are not sure if a prayer that no one understands is worth much.

This is a legitimate concern, but as God says in His Word through the apostle Paul, "For one who speaks in a tongue speaks not to men but to God; for no one understands him, but he utters mysteries in the Spirit" (1 Corinthians 14:2). Just as there are many languages on earth, there is also a heavenly language that the Spirit understands. He longs to fill your mouth with it, helping you better hit the target when you are praying for your needs and the needs of others. This fulfills Christ's promise to send you a "Helper." As Paul also wrote, "Likewise the Spirit helps us in our weakness. For we do not know what to pray for as we ought, but the Spirit himself intercedes for us with groanings too deep for words" (Romans 8:26).

So we see that not only do we sometimes not understand ourselves or even know what we are praying when we pray in the Spirit; oftentimes, we also do not understand what to pray even when we are trying to pray in English (or whatever our native language is). We need the Spirit's help all of the time to pray! "For my thoughts are not your thoughts, neither are your ways my ways," God tells us in Isaiah 55:8. Yet as the Helper prays *through* us, we pray a perfect prayer. Not only do we not get in God's way; we also roll out the red carpet for more expedient answers.

8. You say that Jesus did not discuss speaking in tongues, so it doesn't interest you.

Actually, Jesus did discuss it! He said in Mark's gospel that these signs will accompany those who believe: "In my name they will cast out demons; they will speak in new tongues; they will pick up serpents with their hands; and if they drink any deadly poison, it will not hurt them; they will lay their hands on the sick, and they will recover" (Mark 16:17–18). Speaking in tongues is not a foreign concept to Jesus, and it should not be one to you. It is merely the language of heaven—a language that you need to employ!

9. You are not sure what praying in tongues will do for you practically, and you are fine with your regular prayer life.

The truth is, praying in tongues is much more than just a prayer tool. It bolsters your faith. Praying in a heavenly language calls down heaven on your behalf. And as you begin to see those results, it turns your faith into a supernatural force to be reckoned with! When Scripture tells us that, as the beloved, you and I are to be "building yourselves up in your most holy faith and praying in the Holy Spirit" (Jude 1:20), God is describing how praying in tongues literally makes our faith *holy*. And why not, since it is the Holy Spirit's language? So we should pray in the Spirit on all occasions, as the Word says: "And pray in the Spirit on all occasions with all kinds of prayers and requests. With this in mind, be alert and always keep on praying for all the Lord's people" (Ephesians 6:18 NIV). While God loves the other "regular" prayers you pray, He loves partnering with you to accomplish more in your situation as you allow Him to show you things you otherwise would not have known how to pray. And this often comes when praying in the Spirit. Remember Jeremiah 33:3: "Call to me and I will answer you, and will tell you great and hidden things that you have not known."

10. You are unsure about interpreting when you pray in the Spirit.

As silly as this one sounds, it was not silly to me once upon a time, when I was first learning about this topic and I thought that I would be in serious trouble with God if I did not immediately have an interpretation every time I prayed in tongues. I was basing this on the passage that discusses praying in tongues this way: "But if there is no one to interpret, let each of them keep silent in church and speak to himself and to God" (1 Corinthians 14:28). What Paul is describing here, however, is what is best in a corporate setting. But when you are alone and are employing Spirit prayer, you are speaking to God directly and need not fear doing it wrong. Be at peace. I often find, in fact, that the more I relax and just sit and pray in the Spirit, the more God will begin quickening my mind with what to pray in English, or with a word of encouragement or prophecy for someone else (or myself). That then becomes the interpretation, and trust me, these times of practicing the presence of God in this manner and employing Spirit prayer bear great and lasting fruit—both in your life and in the lives of those you pray for!

11. You are open to the baptism in the Holy Spirit and have asked and asked for it, but it has not happened yet.

If you have asked for the Holy Spirit, then you have Him! As Luke 11:13 tells us, "How much more will the heavenly Father give the Holy Spirit to those who ask him!" So shift your perspective and instead thank God that He *has* given you His Holy Spirit. Then ask Him to just let that gift be made manifest in your new prayer language. Be patient, but persistent. If praying in tongues does not happen right away, treat its pursuit less like a hobby and more like a full-time job. Immerse yourself in deep worship, during which you use your voice in praise and prayer. Stay available. And I know this sounds odd, but take yes for an answer. Never assume that God has given everyone else this gift and not you. You have asked Him for bread, and He will not give you a stone.

12. You are waiting to receive a full vocabulary of this new spiritual language all at once and it has not come, leaving you feeling doubtful and occasionally discouraged.

In the same way in which you did not start speaking your native language in full sentences as a toddler, neither are you expected to do so with your prayer language. In fact, with me, I heard a few syllables in bed one night and felt God telling me to repeat them, so I did. It felt so awkward, the same way I suppose it felt in 1979 when my toddler nephew was trying to say "Granny" to my mother and it came out "Gaggy"! We all tried to get him to perfect it, but Mama was pleased as punch. It was original. Her first grandchild had spoken to her, and nothing else mattered. Before long, Mama was cross-stitching these two precious syllables on everything that would sit still, and we all just knew that she was now and would forever be "Gaggy" to all subsequent grandchildren (and she still is now, forty-plus years later).

So do not despise small beginnings. God is thrilled that you are learning from Him. He loves your two or three syllables. Mine served me well for months and even helped spare my life twice during that time. (I believe those times were directly related to my beginning to employ this prayer tool.) Then one night, I was watching Christian television and my life changed entirely. The minister asked for those who wanted the baptism of the Holy Spirit to come forward at his church, so I got down on my knees right where I was, in my living room. I had asked plenty of times, but I was not too proud to ask again. I went to offer up my few little syllables that I had heard all those months ago, but this time as I began to pray them, *woosh*—the Holy Spirit fell upon me, and I felt as if a river was pouring into the top of my brain and coming directly out of my mouth! With it was an entirely new language that

I could not contain, control or comprehend. But I was different. I was stronger. I was invincible! And I have never—not once—lost that feeling, to this day.

Even now, I cry thinking of that encounter. In fact, right now I am sitting mere feet away from where it happened. Come to think of it, where I am sitting is *exactly* where the TV was sitting that night. In other words, I am now the minister in this very spot, *inviting you* to come forward to receive the baptism of the Holy Spirit. I am eager for you to pray this chapter's life-changing prayers. I am praying that you will! I prayed for you just this morning.

Again, answer the following questions and save them for when you finish the book. At that time, use today's answers for Day 8 of my "10 Days to a Lifetime of Deeper Sleep and Dreams" program at the close of chapter 10. At the end of that day, a link will be provided that guides you to a good-night video where I pray a blessing over your sleep and dreams.

QUESTIONS AND PRAYER

1. Name two things that prevent you from spending more time in prayer.

2. Name two blockages you may have to the baptism of the Holy Spirit, or to spending more time in Spirit prayer.

Pray this out loud: *Dear precious Holy Spirit, I am realizing there were so many times when You beckoned me to stop and pray, and I ignored You. Forgive me. I never want You to stop beckoning! I speak to the reasons stated that prevent me from praying more, and I ask You to clear the way for me to have uninterrupted, undistracted time with just You each day. I am showing my doubt the door. I serve the God of the impossible! And Holy Spirit, I know there will be times that I do not know what to pray and will need to learn to rely more upon Spirit prayer. O God, baptize me with Your Holy Spirit, according to Your Word! Teach me to use this new language to confound my enemies and to see the will of God brought forth in my life! [If you "hear" any syllables as you pause in prayer here or in the days to come, speak them. Let the Holy Spirit give you utterance. Trust Him, and just as when you prayed for salvation, exercise faith with this type of prayer.] Before long, I know that the River of God will run through me and fill me to overflowing. Thank You for what You are creating in me, Lord: expectancy, faith and discernment! In Jesus' name, Amen!*

THE ALARM CLOCK
BESIDE YOUR BED

You have read the writing on the wall in the previous chapter and have confronted many things in order to bring lasting change to your life. But now that the lights are likely out for the night, let's face facts: Tomorrow will come with its own new challenges, and you must get a plan *now* for how you will react.

Just as you can count on your alarm clock by your bed, or on your phone, to sound its alarm at a pre-set time, you can count on the fact that stress will sound its own alarms in your life every day. You can and should order your life in such a way that the chance of suffering a constant train wreck of chaos and stress is less likely. Yet even then, there will be the predictable "unknowns"—the stressors that are tomorrow's triggers, the boundaries that you are questioning and the changes that you know you are in need of making.

Unlike your alarm clock or phone, which are programmed and predictable, stressful situations arising from these different areas are not. What *is* predictable is how you will decide to respond to them, and how you will choose to filter them so that you are not swimming in their aftermaths all day long. The person who swims in the aftermath of stress all day long is surely a person who will never give it to God and go to bed.

Stressors—Setting a Plan for Tomorrow

How can you make sure you are ready for tomorrow's stress triggers? Try these three important steps, all of which begin with the letter *A*: acknowledgment, assignment and alignment.

Step 1—Acknowledgment

Recognize that this situation has passed through God's hand to you. Not that He is the originator of bad things—Scripture shows us that He is not that type of Father. But He also was not on vacation when it happened, as I like to say. He allowed it, and you must ask yourself why. Finding the answer to that mystery brings the very purpose you need in order to overcome the problem.

All such *Why?* questions in your life lead you to give God your undivided attention and hear His voice more clearly. They are intended to strengthen you, not stress or distress you. First, stop and acknowledge that this stressful situation you are facing passed through God's hand to you, and then ask Him why. Job did it. Jesus did it. Now you must do it.

You may not hear an audible voice in reply, but you will likely have a thought that you have never had before about the situation. You will see it in a new way and gain a different perspective. Stay in that place and allow God's still, small voice to speak to you. It will not be confusing or complicated. But it will likely bring an "aha" moment in which you feel as if a small night-light has lit a clear path for you. And sometimes, there will be such a flood of illumination that it brightens everything for you instantly, starting with your mood.

Step 2—Assignment

In that place, if God shows you why He allowed a heartache or challenge to pass through the filter of His hand to you, you then have your assignment—to put faith to what you heard and make the changes necessary to avoid such a situation again.

For instance, let's say you are stressed out because you cannot pay your bills. But let's say that you cannot pay your bills because you quit your job hastily over an offense from a co-worker. In that case, God might tell you to think twice before making such a rash decision again. Your assignment would then be to choose growth. Although doing so does not instantly pay your bills that very day, it does bring the instant peace that comes with obedience to God (which will lead to the provision you need, I assure you).

But what do you do if a stress or trial is no direct fault of your own—like when a spouse leaves you? You must still ask your heavenly Father for His perspective. Go back long before your mate's departure and ask God if He had released you to marry this person to begin with. If the answer is yes, a peace should wash over you that lets you know that you are in step with God's will and that He is on the scene to fight for you (as you keep your heart clear and free of unforgiveness). God may or may not show you at that moment that your marriage will be restored, but the peace you receive will allow you to give it to God and go to bed that night.

If the answer to your question is no, the marriage was not God's plan for you, that does not release you from the vow you made to your spouse, but it could explain the strife. Or perhaps the Lord might bring to mind ways that you failed to fulfill your vows to your mate, along with ways to make changes and even make amends.

The point is that in both of those last examples, there is once again the assignment and invitation for growth. It does not bring your spouse back that night, but it does bring the peace and the hope you need, which in turn will bring a better night's sleep.

What do you do if you ask God the *Why?* question and you do *not* get an answer at all, or any assignment in response? It happens to all of us at one point or another, which leads us to step 3, alignment.

Step 3—Alignment

Once you have taken your stressful situation to God, have asked Him why He allowed it to pass through His hand to you, and perhaps have heard nothing but crickets, it could be that you are out of earshot of God's voice. He might be talking, but it is as if you and God are on completely different radio frequencies. You must get back to the channel on which you once heard Him.

Think back to a time when you felt closest to God, and decision-making was peaceful and stress free. What were you doing differently during that time? Has your connection with other believers lessened since then? Have those people been replaced with friends who deprioritize the Holy Spirit or the resulting holiness that comes from a close walk with Him? Are you spending less time in God's Word or in prayer? If so, get realigned with Him. Get back to your "first love," which, by the way, is not some phrase from a 1960s summer fling movie. It comes straight from the book of Revelation as Christ is addressing the seven churches:

> He might be talking, but it is as if you and God are on completely different radio frequencies. You must get back to the channel on which you once heard Him.

I know your works, your labor, your patience, and that you cannot bear those who are evil. And you have tested those who say they are apostles and are not, and have found them liars; and you have persevered and have patience, and have labored for My name's sake and have not become weary. Nevertheless I have this against you, that you have left your first love. Remember therefore from where you have fallen; repent and do the first works, or else I will come to you quickly and remove your lampstand from its place—unless you repent.

Revelation 2:2–5 NKJV

If you cannot seem to hear any divine direction when you pray about your stressors and attempt to give them to God, do not jump up and run away, phone a friend, get a snack or whatever else you are tempted to get up and reach for. Press in. Be patient. It is in this season of uncertainty that you need a prophetic directional dream from God more than ever. If you do not quiet yourself in His presence, you may never get to sleep, stay asleep and reach the deep sleep necessary to accomplish the sleep cycles that physiologically lead to dreaming. Stay put. Invest in your spirit. Consider a food fast to feed your inner "spirit man" with extra listening prayer. I offer fasting ideas in my ebook *A Hunger for God: Your Personal Guide*

to Prayer and Fasting. You can find it (no charge!) at view.publitas
.com/laura-harris-smith-ministries/a-hunger-for-god-fasting-ebook
/page/1.

I once did a teaching called "A Diet of the Mind." In fact, I
almost wrote a book by that title, and may still one day. I have
used the same illustration in sermons and devotionals, and I even
did an online devotional on it one time (which you can see here,
again at no charge: https://youtu.be/7tPrdoigrU4). In this teaching, I take a stalk of celery and let it soak overnight in a glass of
water filled with red food coloring. Within just a few moments,
the discoloration begins to travel up the stalk. By morning, even
the leaves on the end are turning red. It is quite a sight to see.
The reason I bring it up is actually to encourage you to feed on
God's Word and saturate your mind with what His voice sounds
like so you will recognize it when He speaks to you outside His
written Word.

You need to meditate on God's Word—reading and rereading
a passage until the Holy Spirit illuminates it to you. If you will do
this, you will soon find yourself thinking differently about your
circumstances, your relationships and even yourself. And what
you think is what you become. Proverbs 23:7 (KJV) tells us, "As he
[a man or anyone] thinketh in his heart, so is he."

God's Word is also one of the last things to meditate on as you
drift off to sleep, because I have found that it makes for crystal-clear
dreams. Here is a good verse to tuck yourself in with each night.
Speak it over yourself, and command your mind to be subject to
your spirit and only receive the dreams that God intends:

> Finally, brothers, whatever is true, whatever is honorable, whatever
> is just, whatever is pure, whatever is lovely, whatever is commend-

able, if there is any excellence, if there is anything worthy of praise, think about these things.

Philippians 4:8

Questioning Boundaries—Mapping Out Your Goals

Chris and I work from home. Or you could say it this way: We live at our office. We have lived in this house for 30 years, and it is where we have raised 6 children, welcomed 11 grandchildren, run our businesses, where I have written all 25 of my books, where Chris runs all the inner workings of the church government of Eastgate, and it is even where Eastgate was born in our living room (a home birth)! We are in our home 24 hours a day, and we are together 24 hours a day. That is 1,440 minutes a day and 10,080 minutes a week. Of course, we do leave from time to time, but my point is that the many things we do get done from right here!

One of the things we started doing in 2019, to break up blocks of our time, switch gears and force ourselves into a place of relaxation, was to stop and watch a movie—something totally mindless—or find some sort of television series where we can watch one episode at a time. We found one on the History Channel that served its relaxing purpose for about five minutes before I knew it would become a sermon. Or something to write about. Whenever I am inspired, I never know if the releasing of that inspiration will take the form of a book I write, a sermon I deliver or a show episode I film. This time it was two out of three, and I knew it almost instantly. The show we were watching was called *How the States Got Their Shapes*, a fascinating series about each state's borders and how every line on our American map has a story. I would make you sit and watch the whole episode that I watched if I could, but instead, I have edited the information into a few talking points because I think it is relevant to our discussion here about your life, starting tonight.

The show, hosted by Brian Unger and based on Mark Stein's book *How the States Got Their Shapes* (Harper Paperbacks, 2016), is the clash of history, geography and civics classes. But when you add Sunday school and a little bit of psychology to that, it really gets interesting! The story of how each American state got its shape—due to twelve distinct factors that determined its borders—made me mindful of how the borders a person puts around his or her life can determine the shape of the future and whether or not the person's dreams get fulfilled.

We are spending a substantial amount of time talking about nighttime dreams, but for a moment let's talk about the dreams that happen while you are awake—the goals you have for your life and future. Just as our states, countries and continents must have borders for the basic purposes of identification and definition, so must your life. And just as America's past geographical decisions determined her future, your past circumstances will determine your "borders," too, if you let them. But it is far better to let God set the borders that define your life, which will even define your path each day. He is the one with the map for your life.

So what were those twelve things that formed our state borders? Of significance is that at one point, each of these factors was a barrier. A red territory challenge. As we go through these things, you will see quickly the parallel of how such barriers can form the borders of your life. God has set the borders of your life to be spacious and roomy, and to allow for plenty of adventure. But the enemy has borders of his own planned for you, borders with which to restrict you and make you think you are entirely incapable of fulfilling your destiny. Let's take a quick look at the twelve factors the show about the states mentions, which can also apply to your borders and mine.

1. Water—In the days before modern transportation, highways and airplanes, everyone traveled by water. That's right, water was not just water. It was the source of all commerce, transportation, economy and life. In fact, you may have wondered when you look at a map why all the states on the right side have squiggly borders, while all the states out West resemble boxes. This is because in the eastern half of the country, state borders were formed by waterways in America's infancy. With the advent of the railroads, however, states were marked out by train tracks, which happened in the western half of the country.

Application: Think about the waterways in your life—specifically, the hurts that hurt so badly that you actually cried a river (or wanted to). That river formed a border that your heart said you would never cross again. It became a "state" of mind for you. Today, I speak over you Revelation 21:4 (KJV): "And God shall wipe away all tears from their eyes; and there shall be no more death, neither sorrow, nor crying, neither shall there be any more pain: for the former things are passed away."

2. Demands—Although life was often rugged and dangerous right by the waterways, living there was necessary for the early Americans. It made travel more accessible, not to mention offered water for drinking, washing and bathing. The settlers would even risk making themselves vulnerable to the dangers of flooding to build their settlements along the riverbanks, all due to their demand for a steady water supply.

Application: Some people in your life, despite knowing where your boundaries and borders are, demand that you build your life in a vulnerable and sometimes dangerous place. Maybe it is a boss you cannot get away from who becomes a constant source of stress. Maybe it is a bad marriage that becomes a constant flow of sorrow you cannot escape. Or abuse. Or neglect. If you are hemmed in on all sides by stress and sorrow, I speak Psalm 30:5 (NKJV) over you: "Weeping may endure for a night, but joy comes in the morning."

3. Wars—In early America, foreign players—Spain, France, England—made decisions that started wars. They also slaughtered many Americans whose only choice was to comply or die. Many of our borders were therefore formed due to foreign influence.

Application: What are the wars in your life? How have foreign influences that have no regard for God's calling on your life shaped it? Become a warrior in the wars of your life. In your future battles, I speak Ephesians 6:11 (NIV) over you: "Put on the full armor of God, so that you can take your stand against the devil's schemes."

4. People—Just as the wars in early America were caused by foreign influences, each of those wars could be directly traced back to a person of authority—a gatekeeper who pushed the boundaries of his or her jurisdiction.

Application: You just identified the wars in your life in number 3; now ask yourself, *Who are the people in authority who are drawing a line wherever they want in my life, outside the will of God?* You do not want ungodly authority in your life. God *does* want authority figures in your life, but not ungodly players who are calling the shots and costing you your life, one dissatisfied day at a time. Sometimes you can escape these relationships quickly, and sometimes you are bound by God and by man's law. If this is you, I speak over you Romans 12:19–21 (NIV):

> Do not take revenge, my dear friends, but leave room for God's wrath, for it is written: "'It is mine to avenge; I will repay,' says the Lord." On the contrary:
> "If your enemy is hungry, feed him; if he is thirsty, give him something to drink. In doing this, you will heap burning coals on his head."
> Do not be overcome by evil, but overcome evil with good.

5. Religious Differences—Maryland's lines were drawn for Catholics ("Mary" land), Pennsylvania's for Quakers, and Delaware's semicircle top was to buffer Delaware's Dutch from the Pennsylvania Quakers.

Application: I want to challenge the religious borders you have put around your relationship with Jesus Christ. He is not Baptist or Methodist or even white American. I speak over you here Ephesians 4:5–6 (NIV): "One Lord, one faith, one baptism; one God and Father of all, who is over all and through all and in all." I also challenge you to find a Bible-believing, Spirit-led Christian church that does not put borders around your worship. Remember 2 Corinthians 3:17 (NIV): "Now the Lord is the Spirit, and where the Spirit of the Lord is, there is freedom."

6. Divisions—Every early American border marked by a surveyor caused division. It took land from one person and gave it to another, and if you fell on the wrong side, you could very well be living in a different state within seconds.

Application: This is a more interpersonal/intrapersonal comparison I am making, as opposed to wars between more corporate players of authority. It has to do with the divisions in your relationships and the borders they set for you emotionally. You can only say so much about a particular topic with a particular family member before it triggers a very predictable response. Perhaps it is religion or politics. You have to steer clear of this topic or else you get a predictable reaction. Learning about these landmines may have caused you to withdraw your heart from a relationship long ago. If you did that out of fear, confront it in your heart. But if you did that to preserve the relationship for the sake of peace, then I bless you with Romans 12:18 (NASB): "If possible, so far as it depends on you, be at peace with all people."

7. Compromises—Have you ever heard of the 36-30 Line? The Missouri Compromise of 1820 instituted the 36°30′ parallel as the northern limit for where slavery was legal in the Western territories. As part of this compromise, Maine (which was formerly part of Massachusetts) was admitted as a free state.

Application: Circa 2012, someone gave me a prophetic word: "No more disappointments." And the person added, "I'm not sure if it's that you are never going to be disappointed again, or if it's that you are just going to lower your expectations and avoid disappointment." Turns out it was the latter. I didn't even know I had done it in two specific relationships, until God sent two new people into my life who helped me see that my previous high expectations *were from God*. He didn't want me to compromise. But I had, and while it is true that it had spared me from disappointment, I see now that it had also resulted in failing to aim for God's best in these types of relationships. I had held back due to fear. Do not let compromise form the scars on the map of your life. Like the government's 36-30 Line, you must decide which side of the boundary you will live your life on—the side of slavery or the side of freedom. Remember John 8:36 (NIV): "So if the Son sets you free, you will be free indeed."

8. Slavery—As I previously stated, the issue of slavery influenced the formation of many of the borders for the early American states.

Application: What are you enslaved to? Addiction? Fear? Rejection? Abuse? These are forming borders around your life that are holding you back. Be delivered today! Remember Galatians 5:1: "For freedom Christ has set us free; stand firm therefore, and do not submit again to a yoke of slavery."

9. Finances—The discovery of gold caused many states to fight for the gold mines to be included within their territories. California was among these, and greed formed its borders. (History has repeated itself there, defining California as a state that appears to have everything but is often viewed as financially and morally bankrupt.) Other states drew their lines to exclude the gold. Washington let Idaho have some territory just to get rid of the crazy, unruly prospectors. Same for Nebraska and Kansas; they chose peace over greed.

Application: This analogy is not meant to suggest that you cannot be wealthy. But wealth cannot be what defines the borders of your life, or when you go to relax, you will struggle with feelings of failure. I speak over you Matthew 6:24: "No one can serve two masters, for either he will hate the one and love the other, or he will be devoted to the one and despise the other. You cannot serve God and money."

10. The Prospectors—And what about those unruly prospectors? They had such a wild side that it even affected how the early states defined their borders, sometimes just to be rid of them.

Application: In your case, the "unruly prospectors" are those people whom the enemy plants in your life to confuse your borders. If this applies to your situation, here is my advice for you from Psalm 109:2–4: "For wicked and deceitful mouths are opened against me, speaking against me with lying tongues. They encircle me with words of hate, and attack me without cause. In return for my love they accuse me, but I give myself to prayer."

11. New Inventions and Transportation—As we discussed earlier, most of the Midwest and Western states acquired a boxy feel because, due to the railroads, they formed their borders in perfect lines.

Application: These boxy borders remind me of the coping mechanisms you adopt to get from one place to another in your mind. They are your emotional transports. Once you learned of them, you invented new and faster ways to get where you wanted to go. But in doing so, you were a bit too hasty and strayed from the more natural borders that make you *you*. And maybe living in that fast lane caused you to become a bit too free in forming these new borders however you wanted. So in keeping with our analogies, waterways (tears) are no longer forming your borders and limitations, but you hop on some train that tells you that you can do whatever you want—with no restraints or definition—which is just as dangerous. Then you wind up in a box, like the boxy Midwest states!

Try to identify all your coping mechanisms and get rid of those modes of transportation, trusting God for His design for your borders. Amen? Remember Jeremiah 29:11 (NIV): "'For I know the plans I have for you,' declares the LORD, 'plans to prosper you and not to harm you, plans to give you hope and a future.'"

12. Mountains—Whole mountain ranges divide one state from another in this country. In the case of Virginia and West Virginia, that dividing line marked out the difference between wealth and poverty.

Application: So it is with you. The mountains in your life will either make or break you. You will either learn to scale them, or you will set up camp at their bases and never advance toward your destiny in life. If you are one of those people who feel as if your life has been defined by climbing uphill, I want to remind you that you serve a mountain-melting God. Remember Mark 11:23 (NIV): "Truly I tell you, if anyone says to this mountain, 'Go, throw yourself into the sea,' and does not doubt in their heart but believes that what they say will happen, it will be done for them."

What has defined the boundaries for your life? Who has laid the blueprints for your life? Take time to write these things down when you reach the end of this chapter. That exercise will be very useful to you during the 10-Day program coming up after chapter 10. It is time for you to reset the boundaries for your life according to God's map for you, and that divine map will establish your state of mind for your longer journey.

Discipline and Detoxing—Making the Changes You Need

One final thing to consider as you prepare yourself for tomorrow (and every tomorrow) is the discipline it will take for you to fulfill the dreams and goals you have for your life. One of these areas of discipline is discovering that you were made in the image of a Triune God so that you can remain healthy—body, mind and spirit.

I never tire of reminding people that they were literally made by the Trinity. You see the Trinity on the scene in the Garden of Eden, in the creation of man and woman. Consider Genesis 1:26 (emphasis added): "Then God said, 'Let *us* make man in *our* image, after *our* likeness.'" Who is that *us* and *our*? It is the Father, Son and Holy Spirit. Just as the Trinity has three parts, so do you, and just as His three parts are actually one, so are yours. It is impossible to segregate your three parts when a crisis arises and just treat one part.

In other words, if you get sick and only treat your body—neglecting to address the psychological reasons you may be working yourself into the ground, or the spiritual reasons that cause you not to trust God and to feel as though you must overwork yourself—then you are only treating one-third of yourself. Or if you get sick and you pray and improve your diet, but you never pause to ask God to show you the emotional woundings that are opening the door to sickness in your life, you are still only treating two-thirds of yourself.

If you want to be whole, you must nourish all three parts of yourself! Sometimes it has been so long since we have done it that we need a reset button. A total temple detox.

You are made of three parts: body, mind and spirit, but it is for good reason that your body and mind are the first to show the telltale symptoms of needing a "total self" detox. The reason is because these are the two parts of yourself that interact with others. These two parts can quickly become contaminated if your interactions are unhealthy, such as the ones with the friends you keep or the foods you choose.

If you want to be whole, you must nourish all three parts of yourself!

What's the number-one sign that you need to detoxify? Let's start with your body. You know you need a body detox when you are replacing your recommended nine daily servings of fruits or vegetables with a compromised diet. There is no way your body can function with vitality if you are not supplying it with vital foods. That means eating colorful "living foods" several times a day, as opposed to consuming processed foods, fast foods or junk foods, also known as "dead foods."

What are living and dead foods? Living foods are those that line the outer walls of your grocery store and have to be refrigerated, such as produce, meats and dairy. Dead or processed foods are everything in between. Aisle after aisle of boxes, bags and cans full of foods that can survive weeks (or longer) without refrigeration because they are loaded with preservatives. If we would all shop along the peripherals of our stores, where the electrical plugs are, we would be healthier.

If the foods you eat come mostly from the center of your grocery store and you have very little fresh produce in your cart when you check out, then you are on the fast track toward a health crisis. It is just a matter of *when* it happens, not *if*. As a result of eating a compromised diet, you are tired or overweight, with a sluggish metabolism. Or you have an immune system that is not fighting off seasonal colds or flus or, even worse, chronic illness. This absence of dietary fruits and vegetables and the presence of weight gain or health loss is the number-one sign that you need a body detox.

What are the signs that you need an emotional or mind detox? You find yourself stressed out or easily angered, depressed or just overwhelmed. You sigh a lot and experience what psychologists call "air hunger." And chronic stress can trigger the hormone cortisol, which results in extra belly fat or other more serious chronic health issues. What we jokingly call "love handles" can actually be a sign of a love loss in your life, or at least a sign of stressful relationships.

Look at your relationships the same way as you do your foods: living or dead. Are your friendships those that bring you and your dreams encouragement and life, or mainly doubt and death? You should choose "living relationships," meaning that you deliberately surround yourself with people who are full of hope, light and love. We all cross paths with challenging naysayers from time to time, but if your life's shopping cart is full of deadly relationships, you are on a fast track toward an emotional crisis. Again, it is a matter of *when*, not *if*.

Your spirit is the invisible, eternal thread that holds together your body and mind. Your spirit is also of great benefit to you when you are cleansing both body and mind, often through prayer and reflection. In my book *The 30-Day Faith Detox: Renew Your Mind, Cleanse Your Body, Heal Your Spirit* (Chosen Books, 2016), I connect your bodily ailments with possible emotional toxins, and I offer counseling and coordinating body detoxes to cleanse both. For example, on days 19–24 of the 30-Day program, I have you examine the potential "Relationship Toxins" of your life. On day 19, you do a daily reading that confronts the times when you may have felt betrayed or rejected. With a three-pronged approach, your body and mind are "detoxed" as I lead you through the process of forgiveness, toward a heart healing. We end with a coordinating body detox that contains heart-healthy foods to cleanse your cardiovascular system (such as the "Heart Beet Berry Smoothie"). By the end of the book, you will have accomplished a total body detox of all fifteen major body systems.

We discussed in chapter 8 how sometimes when we feel as if we are waiting on God, He is actually waiting on us. Maybe the ball is in your court to get disciplined and change unhealthy habits in your body, mind or spirit.[1] You are too young to feel this old!

The last few chapters have been intense. You have cleaned out the junk under your bed, faced the writing on the wall and set that alarm clock by your bed. You are ready to welcome the night with peace and anticipation. I will pray that kind of blessing over you shortly in a good-night video as you go through the 10-Day program, but for now, be prepared to do the following things:

- Inhale and receive an anointing for peaceful rest and constructive conversation with the Holy Spirit through dreams as you sleep.
- Exhale and lay down the burdens of your heart. Make the conscious decision to give them to God and go to bed tonight. Welcome the night by faith and not by sight.
- If you find yourself struggling to get to sleep at night, consider using an essential oil blend such as my Quiet Brain, applied liberally to the brain stem at the base of the neck, just under the hairline.

Again, answer the following questions and save them for when you finish the book. At that time, use today's answers for Day 9 of my "10 Days to a Lifetime of Deeper Sleep and Dreams" program at the close of chapter 10. At the end of that day, a link will be provided that guides you to a good-night video where I pray a blessing over your sleep and dreams.

QUESTIONS AND PRAYER

1. Name one or more ways you can better deal with tomorrow's potential stress.

2. Name two signs that you need a body, mind or spirit detox. (And consider doing *The 30-Day Faith Detox* if you are looking for a good total temple cleanse.)

Pray this out loud: *Wonderful Counselor, You alone can help rid me of the stress I allow myself to operate under. Show me what needs changing in my life, and I vow to You that I will listen and obey. And since the chances are good that those stressors are there because I allowed the wrong things or people to map out the borders of my life, I surrender that map to You and ask You to redesign it. In fact, scrap it and show me Your map of my life. Begin by showing me how to detox my body, mind and spirit so that I might be rid of the faith toxins that try to distract and derail me. My life is in Your hands, O God. My future is Yours to decide. In Christ's name, Amen.*

THE MORNING AFTER
A GOOD NIGHT'S SLEEP

Imagine waking up fully rested regularly, with a prophetic dream to launch your day. Now imagine one day that the combination of a prophetic dream, rest and prayer saves your very life. That is exactly what happened to me during the writing of this book. I would like to close by telling you that very personal story, because I have always asked the Lord to help me teach with my very life. I want to be a prophetic embodiment that others can look at to understand God more clearly. I want to inspire you about how the combination of a prophetic dream and the resulting intercession can save your life.

Nighttime Intervention—When a Dream Saves Your Life

In late summer 2020—after spending the year preparing for my daughter's wedding, shooting season 4 of *theTHREE*, keeping

Eastgate church afloat and thriving during a pandemic, leading a neighborhood court fight against a cell tower built just yards from my home, starting a disaster relief center and food pantry at our church after our community was hit by destructive tornadoes, and laying the groundwork for this book—I found myself in another battle for my life. This time, it was not from too much work and too little sleep. In fact, we did not know what "it" was at all when it all hit the day after the big family wedding. Two prophetic dreams, prayer and multiple remedies saved my life. Without any one of those things, you would not be reading this book right now and I would not be here.

I served Jeorgi as her matron of honor (running around in heels all day), and Chris and I threw the big party/reception afterward as the parents of the bride, where I danced for an hour like a teenager. Then I went home happy and healthy. So I thought. I had had a urinary tract infection (UTI) the week before, but I had treated it at home naturally, with a natural antibiotic (oil of oregano). By the day of the wedding, I was entirely asymptomatic. But the day after the wedding, I was a shivering, hot mess. As a naturopathic doctor (and long before that, as a mom), I like to let fever do its work and burn out infection. When my younger kids got older, I even started the practice of creating a "fake fever," if they didn't have a real one, by putting them in a hot tub and not letting them out until the thermometer read at least 102 degrees.

After my temp stayed at 103 for a few days, however, I was so weak that I could not sit up and so dehydrated that I could not even lift a straw to my mouth. My typical body temp hovers around 96 degrees, so my 103 feels like your 105. I was writhing in pain. I remember distinctly one night that my every exhale was a moan, but that it somehow comforted me as a sign that I was alive. (It sounds ridiculous unless you have had a fever that high; then you get a pass.) I knew that, due to the COVID-19 panic, no doctor's office would let me even enter their lobby with this fever. I had an arsenal of natural remedies that we were busy experimenting with, but I could tell there was infection in my body. I had also developed a bad backache right over my kidney area. We continued to pray and treat my condition naturally.

Then, on what I think was night number three of all of this, I had an encounter with the Lord. I cannot tell you if it was a dream or a vision or reality, but I was sitting alone with Jesus. I saw myself, feet tucked up under me, barebacked and totally at peace while He was tending to my back. I saw two cut marks plainly on my lower back, over my kidney areas, as if they were marked for removal. That night in real life, the pain was so intense that you could not even touch the skin over my kidneys without me screaming in pain. What we did not yet know was that an E. coli infection had traveled north up the urinary tract and had made its home in the dead-end cul-de-sacs of my kidneys.

Getting medicine to the right spots was next to impossible because of the hidden nature of this organ system. Just before I experienced this encounter with Jesus, Chris had prayed over and gently anointed my kidneys with oils (therapeutic, antibiotic/antiseptic/antibacterial oils such as oregano, clove, cinnamon, wild orange, etc.). Within one hour the swelling was reduced. But I knew the infection would not give up that easily, especially if it had gotten into my bloodstream. That sometimes happens after kidney infections, and it can be fatal (in fact, this kind of complication kills 270,000 people each year in America).

In my dream/vision/visitation, I saw Jesus tying a cloth string around my midriff, over my kidneys—tightly, as if He was making sure they did not come out. The process was not instantaneous (nor has this healing been instant). It took Him a while, but it did not hurt. Then I heard from Him, *I am binding your wounds.*

I opened my eyes and was back in my bed. The pain was entirely gone, although not the fever. I then drifted off to sleep and had a definite warning dream in which I saw myself in the future in a barebacked dress (which I never wear). I saw two faded scars where my kidneys had been removed. I awoke abruptly and knew right then that the enemy was after both my kidneys—and thus after the longevity of my life. I clung to the first encounter, where I had seen Jesus binding my wounds. Later on, I described this encounter in detail to Nashville artist Laurel Ellsworth, and I commissioned her to paint it.

The next night, after another long and fevered day, I had a startling warning dream that put everything into perspective. The short version is that I was being followed by some men whom I did not know (and whom I interpret to be evil spirits). Once they got me alone, they put a cloth over my head and began to strangle and kill me. I woke up screaming Chris's name, and immediately he awoke and comforted me. While some may say it was a fever-induced nightmare, I say it was a Spirit-induced warning dream. This was when Chris anointed me with the specific essential oils, as I told you about, and prayed for me. I also used homeopathic arnica and silica for the pain, and belladonna for the fever.

We were praying fervently, but we were also asking God to put His super on our natural and alight on these healing medicines He had created for us. I still did not know what was wrong with me, yet the night after the nightmare (so now we were on day five) my foggy brain somehow remembered that I already had an annual checkup scheduled with my ob-gyn for that very next morning. Ah, providence. This doctor is the wonderful man who delivered all six of my kids. I knew he would help me.

I described the previous UTI to him and how I had treated it with naturopathy and homeopathy and was now asymptomatic. But I also told him that I had this horrible backache (which I never do) over my kidneys, so he did a urine culture. That is when we discovered the E. coli. It had apparently made its home in my kidneys in the form of a full-blown kidney infection, with a risk of sepsis (which is usually a death warrant). I already had a few of the symptoms of sepsis, although my studies eventually revealed (and then a doctor confirmed) that what I had were not the main symptoms. So with one small prescription, I narrowly avoided a hospitalization.

Everybody has a bit of E. coli in his or her gut, but evidently I had a whole army living in me. We have no idea how I came in contact with it, especially since I do not eat raw meat, do not eat cheese, and do not swim in contaminated water (or drink it), and I am not an elderly person with a compromised immune system. Yet I do eat spinach and greens every day of my life, and they are particularly vulnerable to contamination—even organic produce since runoff from cattle farms can affect fields where this produce is grown. I also was not exhibiting any of the usual E. coli symptoms (which usually affect the intestinal tract where the food passes), but I guess my strong immune system had destroyed it in my gut and I never knew about it. But on exiting the body, somehow some E. coli got into my urinary tract, mimicked the symptoms of a UTI and then traveled north.

> But I beat death. With intercession. With the two prophetic warning dreams. With homeopathy. With naturopathy. With medicine.

But I beat death. With intercession. With the two prophetic warning dreams. With homeopathy. With naturopathy. With medicine. With other things God gave us on the third day of creation, such as essential oils, herbs/teas (dandelion for kidney detoxing) and minerals (magnesium). Jesus did indeed bind my wounds. Just a few days before that, I was telling someone that I had never had a hurricane named after me. The day after my encounter with Jesus, I heard on the news, "Laura strengthens into a hurricane." I knew right then that I was going to regain my strength, and as Hurricane Laura smashed onto the Gulf Shores, my fever broke.

There still were several weeks of bed rest ahead, however. My blood pressure stayed at about 75 over 45. I lost weight, I was weak and I could not stand up without feeling faint. So this gal who claims to hate sleep, considers it a waste of time and never even naps during the day was in bed for weeks, nonstop. I had a manuscript due (this one), but most days I could not even sit up and type. Then one day as I was looking at the book title, I laughed out loud. I was—quite literally—going to have to give this project to God and go to bed! He was going to make me practice what I would be preaching to you, which is that sometimes you must face the reality of your circumstances, pick your battles, release the rest in prayer and take to bed—in my case for weeks. So I did.

At the end of my first week on bed rest, I got a mysterious package in the mail, with no return address. It contained a set of dictation headphones; you just plug them into your computer and talk. Only my family and dearest friends knew what was going on with me at this time, and despite my asking around in person and by email and text, no one confessed to sending them. It was probably Jesus. He knew I would need them. As a result of their arrival, I dictated the bulk of this book using them, even after my recovery. And it is a good thing I emerged strong, because in the coming weeks I would lose my 94-year-old stepfather (who raised me), I would have two kids contract COVID, and my husband would go through his own health scare, also with a risk of sepsis. It seems as though every single night this year I have had to give something to God and go to bed! And didn't it seem as though we all had to do that every single night of 2020?

But on that hard night when I had the encounter with Jesus—in the dark, with Chris by my bedside—I told my husband how I had seen the two cut marks in my back. Chris had a different interpretation. He said that he instantly heard the word *backstabbing*. I was not so sure about that, but I later looked it up and it means "the action or practice of criticizing someone in a treacherous manner while feigning friendship."[1] So without going into detail about the other events of my summer (many of which revolve around the dream I shared in chapter 4 about having to outrun the snake with the head and mouth of a human), let me just say that I also think part of the surgery Jesus was doing on me was that He was binding some of that year's emotional wounds.

I do not even like that phrase *emotional wounds* because I consider myself a pretty forgiving, keep-moving-forward gal, but I guess maybe there was something under the surface that still needed mending. The Lord showed me early on in this ordeal that a pastor sort of functions like a kidney in the Body of Christ—he or she filters the toxins out of the church, resulting in a clearer, cleaner community and environment. So I willingly welcomed the binding of *all* my wounds in what was the very trying summer of 2020—body, mind and spirit. (All of this has given birth to what is already turning out to be a powerful new season at Eastgate, and every Sunday I see it at the full altar, and with all the new visitors I am having to greet. I literally cannot remember all their names. I believe the binding of my wounds was a prophetic picture of the binding of wounds at Eastgate, and the removal of toxins from my body was prophetic, too. I am so thankful for my family at Eastgate Creative Christian Fellowship!)

Now what about you, friend? We have already seen that prophetic dreams can help your life, but now you see that sometimes they can actually save it. I hope you have read this as if your life depends on it, because one day it might! Now let's get you prepared to interpret some of these dreams you are going to start having.

Last Night's Dreams—Symbols and Interpretations

I now would like to give you a taste of my 1,000-symbol dream dictionary to whet your appetite. I cannot list the whole voluminous dictionary here, but I will include 100 of the most common symbols for you. (You can find the entire dream dictionary in my book *Seeing the Voice of God*.)

When I came up with my dream dictionary originally, I felt I should include a Bible verse for each symbol. Scripture does not always include a modern symbol, so sometimes I relied on decades of interpretations that have come through fasting prayer. You will notice that some verse references are in normal (or roman) type, and others are in *italics*. Normal type denotes a symbol that literally appears in Scripture. *Italic* type denotes a symbol that either is not in Scripture, or if it does appear there, has more of a modern interpretation. Note also that you can refer to the Scripture translation of your choice when looking up the verses or passages I have listed, unless I recommend a specific Bible translation for a unique symbol.

All the symbols you see here (and those in my larger, 1,000-plus symbol dictionary) are supported by God's Word. Some come directly from His *logos* (written Word), and some come from His *rhema* (spoken Word), supported by His *logos*. For example, you wouldn't find the symbol of a rearview mirror in Scripture, yet it can be a reminder in a dream from the Lord not to focus on the past, but to keep moving forward. Alongside that interpretation, I would place *Philippians 3:13* in italics since it urges you to forget that which lies behind and look forward to that which lies ahead.

One thing you will not find in my dream dictionary is the word *feeling*. Secular symbol dictionaries often say a symbol reveals how you are *feeling* about this-or-that situation. That is not my goal here, and it should not be yours either. You are familiar with your feelings already, and what you need to know now is what God says about your dream. Pray over the symbols in your dreams and find faith that God is speaking to you as you sleep—after you have given everything to Him and have gone to bed! This dictionary will help bolster your faith.

abandoned car: a stalled or neglected move of God (*Acts 17:28a; Isa. 66:20*)

adultery: spiritual affair/idolatry (James 4:4a); pornography (Matt. 5:28; Exod. 20:14)

airplane: huge move of God—holds many and occupies the heavens; favor (*Isa. 60:8–10*)

angel: messenger (Job 33:23); protectors, guardians, ministering spirits (Heb. 1:14)

arrow: children (Ps. 127:3–4); poisoned arrows are grief (Job 6:2–4); lies (Jer. 9:8)

babies: spiritual infants (1 Cor. 3:1; 1 Pet. 2:2); birthing new things (*Isa. 42:9*)

baking/bakery: producing something; sustenance (Lev. 7:9; James 1:3 NASB)

balding hair: being uncovered—not having adequate prayer or protection (*1 Cor. 11:15*)

basement: to be abased (*Phil. 4:12 KJV*); humility (*Matt. 23:12; Ezra 9:5 NIV*)

bathrooms: cleansing; the "rest room" (*Gen. 18:4; Heb. 4:9*)

birth/labor: announces bringing forth a new thing (*Isa. 42:9*)

building levels: first floor—the natural, physical realm where we live under heaven (John 3:31); second floor—the second heaven, where angels war, fueled by our prayer (*Eph. 3:10*); third floor—the third heaven, where we visit with God in paradise (*2 Cor. 12:2–4*)

cancer: something potentially emotionally deadly that can spread (*2 Tim. 2:17 NLT*)

car (moving): move of God, varying sizes depending on vehicle; ministry (*Acts 17:28a*)

cooking: preparing spiritual food (Luke 10:40; Ezek. 46:24 NIV)

crutches: vices, coping mechanisms (*Prov. 3:5 NIV; 2 Sam. 3:29*)

dam: a blockage (Deut. 22:7 KJV); a barrier (Prov. 17:14 NIV)

death: a need for a spiritual awakening (Eph. 2:5); death to a dream (Heb. 2:14 NIV)

disease/infirmity: literal ailments (Matt. 4:23); sin and sicknesses (Isa. 53:5 NIV)

diving: falling headlong into danger (Ps. 37:24 NASB)

doctor: the Great Physician, Jesus (Jer. 8:22)

dog (growling): a wicked sentinel/guard dog (Ps. 22:16)

eating: consuming spiritual food or truths (Mark 14:22)

emotions: emotions in your dreams are literal (*Gen. 43:30 NLT*)

family (deceased): revealing generational curses or blessings (*Exod. 20:5–6*)

famous people: ponder what they mean to you; research name meaning (*Ezek. 16:15 NLT*)

fire: destruction (Isa. 47:14); continual worship (Lev. 6:12); tested, pure (Zech. 13:9)

fish (fishing): evangelism, being fishers of men (Mark 1:17)

flying: overcoming life's burdens and escaping (*Jer. 48:9 NLT*)

gifts: spiritual gifts or coming reward (1 Cor. 12; 14)

gun: gossiping, slander and words used as weapons (*Ps. 10:7; Isa. 54:17*)

hair: spiritual covering (1 Cor. 11:14–15)

hand: if right, victory, long life (Ps. 20:6); if left, riches, wisdom, honor (Prov. 3:16)

hat: a symbol of authority for women (1 Cor. 11:6); a covering (Exod. 39:28)

homeless person: an evil spirit searching for a home (Luke 8:27 NLT)

Indians: a literal call to prayer for sins against Native Americans (*Isa. 10:2; Job 5:16*)

injury: a spiritual or emotional wounding (Jer. 30:15)

insurance: the need for protection from loss (*Eccles. 7:12*)

jail: circumstantially imprisoned or a loss of freedoms (Gen. 39:20)

judge: one who can decide your fate (James 4:12)

keys: the unlocking of doors of opportunity or progress (Rev. 1:18)

killer: an evil spirit that seeks your life or success (*1 Cor. 15:55*)

kiss/kissing: intimacy (Song 1:1–2; Ps. 2:12)

kitchen: working hard to spiritually nourish others (Luke 10:40)

knees: symbolic of being on your knees in prayer (Eph. 3:14 NKJV; Dan. 6:10 NKJV)

labor: birthing something in life through intense strain (Jer. 6:24)

laundry: airing sin—"dirty laundry" (*Rom. 13:12*); secrets of the heart (1 Cor. 14:25)

left turn: the opposite of a right turn is a "wrong" turn or decision in life (Eccles. 10:2)

lion: Jesus—the Lion of the Tribe of Judah (Ps. 17:12); prowling enemy (1 Pet. 5:8)

luggage: baggage from one's past (*Matt. 11:28*); prepared to move on (*Luke 10:4*)

mailman: a messenger or prophet (2 Kings 19:14)

makeup: covering one's flaws (2 Kings 9:30)

mall: may mean "maladies" (since the root *mal* occurs in many illnesses) and may divulge that the dream is about your health (*Matt. 10:1* YLT)

medal: reward, honor and recognition (*Rev. 22:12* NIV)

mute: presence of a deaf and dumb spirit; cannot speak for self (Matt. 9:33; Mark 9:17–29)

naked: pure (Gen. 2:25; Job 1:21); shame (Isa. 47:3); vulnerable, uncovered (Gen. 9:21)

necklace: a yoke around the neck; a bondage (Ps. 73:6 NIV; Isa. 10:27)

nursing/breastfeed: a call to breastfeed (Isa. 66:11; 1 Thess. 2:7); feed a desire (Ps. 37:4)

obesity: struggling with great, well-fed fleshly desires (*Gal. 5:16*)

ocean: God's deep truths/judgments (Ps. 36:6 NLT); if tossed at sea, immature (Eph. 4:14)

oil: invites anointing (Exod. 29:7); Holy Spirit (1 Sam. 16:13); used for healing (James 5:14)

paralyzed: the enemy is trying to cripple you (John 5:8)

parent: authority (Deut. 5:16); earthly father may = heavenly Father (Heb. 12:10–11)

pen/pencil: the writing gift and the ability to communicate (Ps. 45:1)

police/cop: spiritual authority (1 Pet. 2:13)

purse: wealth or finances (Prov. 7:20 NIV)

Q-tip: the need to clean out one's ears and listen to wisdom (*Isa. 6:10*)

quarterback: leadership under pressure; great responsibility (*Neh. 9:38*)

rainbow: promises God has made to you (Gen. 9:13)

rearview mirror: focusing on the past, not moving forward (*Phil. 3:13*; *Luke 9:62*)

ring: favor, authority and affirmation (Jer. 22:24; Hag. 2:23)

running: the race of life and your journey (Phil. 2:16)

scars: past emotional wounds, hurts (John 20:27)

school: learning; grade level shows difficulty of tests (Matt. 11:29; Acts 19:9 NASB)

sex: may reveal a spirit of lust; if dreaming of a past relationship, break soul ties in prayer (*1 John 3:3*)

shark: a hidden demonic predator; pray prayers of protection if seen in dream (*Isa. 27:1*)

shoulders: shouldering a burden (Gen. 49:15); also government (Isa. 9:6)

snake: Satan (Gen. 3:14a); alcohol/wine (Prov. 23:32); evil-doers (Ps. 140:3)

snow: a call to war/pray seen in a dream or awake; snow heralds war (Job 38:22–23)

telephone: communication—with others, but mainly with God (*Jer. 33:3*)

test: being tested by life's trials (2 Cor. 8:22 NASB); a lesson to learn (Ps. 119:71)

thief: Satan, or one of his spirits sent to steal from you (John 10:10a; Prov. 29:24)

tongue: decides your future; holds the power of life and death (Prov. 18:21; James 3:4–5)

tornado: a warning of coming danger or attack and a call to pray (Ps. 55:8 NASB)

twins: the double-portion anointing on your life (2 Kings 2:9; Job 42:10)

umbrella: personal covering or protection in life's storms (*Ps. 27:5*)

upstairs: the second heaven where we do spiritual warfare prayer; see building levels

vacation: refreshment and rest (*Heb. 4:10*)

vertigo: being out of balance or off-balance (*2 Cor. 8:13* GW)

waking: a need for spiritual awakening (Rom. 13:11)

wallet: wealth or finances (Prov. 7:20 NLT)

water: precedes birth, brings cleansing, implies baptism (Ezek. 16:4; John 3:5; Num. 19:21)

wind: change; God's messenger of change, "the winds of change" (Ps. 104:4 NIV; Eph. 4:14)

window: may be God revealing a "window of opportunity" (Gen. 8:6; 2 Cor. 11:33)

X-ray: having intense perception and spiritual discernment (*Ps. 119:125 NLT*)

yelling: irritating, annoying situations or people (Prov. 27:14)

yoke: a picture of slavery; see necklace

zebra: a black-or-white situation that calls for an unequivocal decision (1 Kings 3:9)

zipper on lips: a sign that you are to keep quiet (*Lam. 3:28*)

zombies: the lost who are dead in sin; the walking dead (*Eph. 2:1–5*)

You have now finished reading the main text of this chapter, although still ahead is the "10 Days to a Lifetime of Deeper Sleep and Dreams" program that you will want to do. In preparation for that, let's first wrap up some final questions as you make your way to a lifetime of deeper sleep and dreams:

QUESTIONS AND PRAYER

1. Name a prophetic dream you have had that may have helped save your life. (If you cannot think of one, be on the lookout, because they will now come!)

2. Name a recurring symbol you often see in your dreams. What might God be saying to you based on the dream dictionary's interpretations?

Pray this out loud: *In the name above all names—Jesus Christ—I dedicate my sleep, my bedroom and my dreams to be God's conference room and the place in which I receive regular instruction and insight. I ask for the patience to "pray into" a dream until I understand it, and the wisdom with which to apply it to my life and be edified. I expect my sleep to improve! I expect to hear from You more! I expect my life to change! I thank You in advance, God, and pray all this by faith. Amen and amen.*

Time for Change—10 Crucial Days

If you have finished reading this book and have completed the questions for all 10 chapters, then you are ready for my "10 Days to a Lifetime of Deeper Sleep and Dreams" program! (If not, please take time to go back and answer any questions you missed. You will be glad you did!) Friend, the next 10 days (since I hope you will begin the program immediately) are crucial for you. They will change the way you sleep and dream. Try to do all 10 days in a row so that you can really see cumulative change. Let's get to it!

Day 1

Today, consider the distractions that prevent you from making that trip down the hallway to your bedroom at a reasonable time each night. A friend once had a vision of a man in a business suit sitting outside my bedroom door, blocking my entrance. I knew immediately that she was seeing a spirit that was trying to keep me working so I would not sleep. Remember that vision for yourself.

Now, referring back to chapter 1 and its questions, allow the Holy Spirit to help you make some important changes. Decide once and for all that you will allow God to pick your battles for you, and identify what they are as they pertain to your stressors, work and worries.

Make sure to go to www.LauraHarrisSmith.com/Goodnight Videos after you process these things, where I will pray a blessing over your sleep and dreams concerning what you learned in chapter 1.

Day 2

Today is all about your bedroom! While this entire book takes place in your bedroom, today you put together a plan for making that room a sanctuary, using the resources and ideas I provided.

So, referring back to chapter 2 and its questions, and with the Holy Spirit's prompting, decide how you will make your bedroom a place of peace and security that is worthy of spending one-third of your life in. (Even if you will not be in this bedroom forever, you are there now and it is worth investing in.) Pray and ask God to speak to you in dreams, if necessary, tonight.

Make sure to go to www.LauraHarrisSmith.com/Goodnight Videos, where I will pray a blessing over your sleep and dreams concerning what you learned in chapter 2.

Day 3

Today is the day you clean out your closet and get a whole new wardrobe!

Refer to chapter 3 and its questions and four steps, and with the Holy Spirit's prompting, identify all the monitoring and familiar spirits in your life. Do not scrimp on today's exercise or the prayers you are being asked to pray there, including the one that invites the Holy Spirit into these now-cleansed spaces. And remember to ask God for that new wardrobe that will affect the way you "**BARE**" your soul with your *B*ehaviors, *A*ttitudes, *R*eactions and *E*xpressions.

Make sure to go to www.LauraHarrisSmith.com/Goodnight Videos, where I will pray a blessing over your sleep and dreams concerning what you learned in chapter 3.

Day 4

Today, you will become convinced that God spoke to His children in Scripture through dreams of guidance and comfort, and that He wants to do the same for you. If you are a son or daughter of God, He is pouring out His Spirit in these last days so that you can dream dreams and see visions.

Refer to chapter 4 and its questions, and with the Holy Spirit's prompting, get your inner intercessor engaged. Implement my ABCs for ZZZs, remembering to do some quick bedtime math by determining what time you need to rise, and then subtracting 8½ hours to ensure an adequate night's sleep.

Also go to www.LauraHarrisSmith.com/GoodnightVideos, where I will pray a blessing over your sleep and dreams concerning what you learned in chapter 4.

Day 5

Today is your day to change the world. Are you convinced yet that you possess that kind of power? If not, you will worry and fret over the global turmoil. But if you can engage in prayer and use your prophetic dreams to help others get on board with you, praying them in (and even using social media to accomplish this, with some of the ideas I provided for you), you will become a true influencer. Remember to limit your television and phone usage just before bedtime since it can interfere with melatonin production and prevent sleepiness.

Refer to chapter 5 and its questions, and with the Holy Spirit's prompting, itemize all of the things in the world around you—politically, environmentally, socially, etc.—that cause you stress or fear. Decide to be a participant in that world through prayer and the interpretation of your prophetic dreams, but not to allow any of it to steal your sleep or peace.

Also go to www.LauraHarrisSmith.com/GoodnightVideos, where I will pray a blessing over your sleep and dreams concerning what you learned in chapter 5.

Day 6

Today, you will do the most important soundcheck of your life. Just as when I am in the studio filming my show, *theTHREE*, and I have to make sure that the director and I have a proper connection to hear one another for a smooth production, you need to never go to bed without checking your connection to God.

Refer to chapter 6 and its questions, and with the Holy Spirit's prompting, let God's voice drown out every other voice in your head, whether it be that of a skeptic or even your own.

Also go to www.LauraHarrisSmith.com/GoodnightVideos,

where I will pray a blessing over your sleep and dreams concerning what you learned in chapter 6.

Day 7

Today might be a difficult day for you in this 10-Day program, but do not shrink back from clearing that junk from under your bed. It all makes for a lumpy mattress!

Refer to chapter 7 and its questions, and with the Holy Spirit's prompting, identify the fears in your life—big and small—along with addictions of any kind. Finally, ask God for His help in illuminating those whom you need to forgive in life, even if one of them is God Himself. And make sure to forgive yourself too, friend.

Then go to www.LauraHarrisSmith.com/GoodnightVideos, where I will pray a blessing over your sleep and dreams concerning what you learned in chapter 7.

Day 8

Today's exercise might very well take place in the dark, as you ask God to make the writing on the wall glow while you are lying in bed.

Refer to chapter 8 and its questions, and with the Holy Spirit's prompting, confront your prayerlessness. End the excuses, and dream about what answered prayer looks like for you in all areas of your life. Then confront your doubts and declare to heaven and hell (which are listening) that you will never lose your faith! Most importantly, ask God to remove all blockages to the baptism of the Holy Spirit . . . and then receive it.

Also go to www.LauraHarrisSmith.com/GoodnightVideos, where I will pray for this baptism for you, as well as a blessing for your sleep and dreams, based on chapter 8.

Day 9

Tonight, you prepare for tomorrow. Since God is already there, He has a plan for every stressor that awaits you. He also knows His plan for your life, which you can most readily identify by looking at the dreams He has planted in your heart for your future.

Refer to chapter 9 and its questions, and with the Holy Spirit's prompting, identify the borders and restrictions that prevent you from carrying out that calling, and then get back on track—body, mind and spirit—perhaps even through a total-temple detox.

Make sure to go to www.LauraHarrisSmith.com/Goodnight Videos, where I will pray a blessing over your sleep and dreams concerning what you learned in chapter 9.

Day 10

The questions you will look back at today are less intensive since chapter 10 merely challenged you to take seriously your prophetic dreams, as if your life depends on them—since one day it just might! Mine did. Compare the symbols in your dreams to the 100 symbols and interpretations I have provided (or to the 1,000-symbol dictionary if you have a copy of *Seeing the Voice of God*). Let the Holy Spirit communicate with you in the night, as you are able to sleep well and dream because you have given it all to God and gone to bed.

Finally, make sure to go to www.LauraHarrisSmith.com/Good nightVideos, where I will pray a final blessing over your sleep and dreams concerning what you learned in chapter 10.

Talk to Me!

Friend, I want to hear your testimony of how you have improved your sleep, increased your dreams and gained a new perspective on prayer while reading this book. Each story will encourage me and someone else who might read it. Please drop me a note at Breakthrough@ LauraHarrisSmith.com, or post your testimony on my Facebook author page at www.Facebook.com/LauraHarrisSmithPage.

And finally, I leave you with a poem to summarize your journey in this book. It is both a prayer and a blessing, and if you choose to read it each night, it can even serve as a declaration you release over yourself. Sweet dreams!

Already There

Today I woke and spent the day as me, myself and I
Depending on the me required, I'm here to satisfy
It all got done, it all got said, and every me endured
But now it's time to lay us down and try to rest assured

Tonight I'll tell my mind to tell my head to get some rest
I'll lay both on my pillow and exhale the strife and stress
My racing thoughts and worries aren't allowed to run
    ahead
It's time to give them all to God and will myself to bed

Tomorrow's not allowed to cheat tonight out of its dreams
My date with rest is not just counting sheep as it would
    seem
For this divine appointment with my God at each day's
    end
Will bring the peace and plan on which tomorrow does
    depend

So silence the distractions down the hall and near this bed
And help me find the treasures in my sleep and dreams
    instead
Tell monsters in my closest they are not allowed to fight

The weapons 'neath my pillow now will put them all to
    flight

The world outside my window will not break in with its
    wars
The voices in my head have all been muted, all but Yours
No hiding junk beneath the bed, my fear and sin are gone
And written on my walls are only words the Spirit's drawn

My clock is set for triumph from the moment I awake
Your grace will lead me to success and through each hard
    mistake
So now I lay me down to sleep with this one final prayer
I do not fear tomorrow. My God's already there.

                      © Laura Harris Smith, December 2020

NOTES

Chapter 1 The Distraction down the Hall

1. Never ignore the telltale symptoms of a true heart attack: shortness of breath, dizziness or nausea, chest pain radiating into your shoulder and arm (usually the left arm), jaw pain or back pain, and sweating. These may be warning signs of a heart attack and not simply stress symptoms.

2. Mayo Clinic Staff, "Stress Symptoms: Effects on Your Body and Behavior," MayoClinic.org, April 4, 2019, https://www.mayoclinic.org/healthy-lifestyle/stress-management/in-depth/stress-symptoms/art-20050987.

3. "The #1 Hospital in the Nation," MayoClinic.org, https://www.mayoclinic.org/about-mayo-clinic/quality/top-ranked.

4. Apple Dictionary, s.v. "stress," Apple Inc., version 2.3.0 (203.16.12), 2005–2018.

5. Susan M. Turley, *Understanding Pharmacology for Health Professionals*, 5th ed. (Upper Saddle River, N.J.: Pearson Education, 2016), 333, Kindle.

6. The National Institute of Mental Health, "Mental Health Medications," accessed April 2, 2021, https://www.nimh.nih.gov/health/topics/mental-health-medications/index.shtml.

7. Turley, *Understanding Pharmacology*, 333.

8. NIMH, "Mental Health Medications."

Chapter 2 The Treasures inside Your Bedroom

1. Blue Letter Bible Lexicon, s.v. "*eirēnē*" (Strong's G1515), https://www.blueletterbible.org/lang/lexicon/lexicon.cfm?t=kjv&strongs=g1515.

2. Again, you can find much more detailed information on each of these sleep stages in my book *Seeing the Voice of God: What God Is Telling You through Dreams and Visions* (Chosen Books, 2014).

3. "Common Sleep Disorders," Cleveland Clinic, last updated December 23, 2020, https://my.clevelandclinic.org/health/articles/11429-common-sleep-disorders.

4. Elizabeth Segran, Ph.D., "The $70 Billion Quest for a Good Night's Sleep," Fast Company, April 30, 2019, https://www.fastcompany.com/90340280/the-70-billion-quest-for-a-good-nights-sleep.

5. You can go to www.NeuromaticsOil.com to learn more about Quiet Brain® oil. Two case studies and countless worldwide testimonies later, relief from insomnia (with the resulting sweet sleep) is the number-one testimony we receive about Quiet Brain oil. There you can also download a free ebook that explains the story and science behind our patented blends.

Chapter 3 The Monsters in Your Closet

1. "Prayer against a Familiar Spirit and Monitoring Spirits," Missionaries of Prayer, April 11, 2015, https://www.missionariesofprayer.org/2015/04/prayer-against-a-familiar-spirit-and-monitoring-spirits/.

2. Ibid.

3. Blue Letter Bible Lexicon, s.v. "*dipsychos*" (Strong's G1374), https://www.blueletterbible.org/lang/lexicon/lexicon.cfm?Strongs=G1374&t=KJV.

Chapter 4 The Weapons under Your Pillow

1. Blue Letter Bible Lexicon, s.v. "*symphōneō*" (Strong's G4856), https://www.blueletterbible.org/lang/lexicon/lexicon.cfm?Strongs=G4856&t=KJV.

2. Blue Letter Bible Lexicon, s.v. "*aiteō*" (Strong's G154), https://www.blueletterbible.org/lang/lexicon/lexicon.cfm?Strongs=G154&t=KJV.

3. Blue Letter Bible Lexicon, s.v. "*pragma*" (Strong's G4229), https://www.blueletterbible.org/lang/lexicon/lexicon.cfm?Strongs=G4229&t=KJV.

Chapter 5 The World outside Your Window

1. You can view the re-release of this prophetic word at https://youtu.be/6175yIyaHE4.

2. "Prophetic Word from Kim Clement for the USA," Cornerstone Fellowship Church, December 29, 2020, http://www.cornerstonefrederick.com/blog/2020/12/29/prophetic-word-from-kim-clement-for-the-usa.

3. Ibid.

Chapter 6 The Voices in Your Head

1. Juliana Kataoka, "15 Answers to the Questions You Ask Yourself at 3 A.M.," BuzzFeed.com, February 19, 2017, https://www.buzzfeed.com/julianakataoka/3-am-questions.

2. Blue Letter Bible Lexicon, s.v. "*didaskō*" (Strong's G1321), https://www.blueletterbible.org/lang/lexicon/lexicon.cfm?Strongs=G1321&t=KJV.

3. Blue Letter Bible Lexicon, s.v. "*hēsychios*" (G2272), https://www.blueletterbible.org/lang/lexicon/lexicon.cfm?t=kjv&strongs=g2272.

4. Blue Letter Bible TR Concordance, s.v. "λαλεῖν" (or "*lalein*," G2980), https://
www.blueletterbible.org/lang/lexicon/inflections.cfm?strongs=G2980&t=KJV
&ot=TR&word=λαλεῖν. See also https://biblehub.com/greek/lalein_2980.htm,
as well as *Liddell and Scott's Greek-English Lexicon* (abridged), s.v. "lalein," and
Malcolm Horlock, "1 Corinthians 14 (3)," https://www.preciousseed.org/article
_detail.cfm?articleID=53.

Chapter 7 The Junk under Your Bed

1. Apple Dictionary, s.v. "addiction."
2. Carey A. Reams with Cliff Dudley, *Choose! Life or Death: The Reams
Biological Theory of Ionization* (Harrison, Ark., New Leaf Press: 1978), 156,
https://christianhealtheducation.com/wp-content/uploads/2017/10/Choose-life
-or-Death.pdf.

Chapter 8 The Writing on the Wall

1. The statistics in this paragraph are taken from Michael Lipka, "5 Facts
about Prayer," Pew Research Center, May 4, 2016, www.pewresearch.org/fact
-tank/2016/05/04/5-facts-about-prayer/.
2. The statistics in this section are taken from CBSNEWS.com staff, "Poll: Do
You Believe in Miracles," CBS News, December 9, 1999, https://www.cbsnews
.com/news/poll-do-you-believe-in-miracles/.
3. Apple Dictionary, s.v. "apostate."
4. Apple Dictionary, s.v. "apostasy."

Chapter 9 The Alarm Clock beside Your Bed

1. If you have been seeking a reset button for your body, mind and spirit, sign
up for my 30-Day Faith Detox challenge, free with the purchase of the book by the
same title on my website: www.LauraHarrisSmith.com/30dayfaithdetoxchallenge.

Chapter 10 The Morning after a Good Night's Sleep

1. Apple Dictionary, s.v. "backstabbing."

Laura Harris Smith is a certified nutritional counselor and naturopathic doctor with three degrees in Original Medicine. But before all of that, she was just a farmer's daughter with a love for colorful food and a pastor's granddaughter with a heart to see others prosper spiritually. Laura and her husband, Chris, are the founding co-pastors of Eastgate Creative Christian Fellowship near Nashville, Tennessee, where they specialize in helping people get healthy—body, mind and spirit—believing it is the only path to wholeness.

In television for more than fifty years, Laura is the executive producer and host of *theTHREE*, her body, mind and spirit show that airs every day of the week all over the world. Laura is also the CEO and inventor of Neuromatics® Oil, which is home to her patented essential oil blends of Quiet Brain®, Happy Brain® and Sharp Brain® products.

Laura is the author of more than 25 books and ebooks, including *The 30-Day Faith Detox: Renew Your Mind, Cleanse Your Body, Heal Your Spirit* (Chosen, 2016), *The Healthy Living Handbook: Simple, Everyday Habits for Your Body, Mind and Spirit* (Chosen, 2017), *Get Well Soon: Natural and Supernatural Remedies for Vibrant Health* (Chosen, 2019), and *Seeing the Voice of God: What God is Telling You through Dreams and Visions* (Chosen, 2014).

Married for 37 years, Laura and Chris have six adult children: Jessica, Julian, Jhason, Jeorgi, Jude and Jenesis, all homeschooled, all writers and all gifted communicators. With two-thirds of these kids now grown and married, "the grandmuffins" now far outnumber the kids.

Invite Laura to speak: booking@LauraHarrisSmith.com
Official website: www.LauraHarrisSmith.com
Television: www.theTHREE.tv
Neuromatics Oils: www.NeuromaticsOil.com
Chris and Laura's Nashville church: www.EastgateCCF.com
Facebook: Facebook.com/LauraHarrisSmithPage
Twitter: @LauraHSmith

More from
Laura Harris Smith

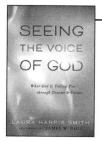

With absorbing insight, *Seeing the Voice of God* demystifies nighttime dreams and daytime visions, revealing the science behind the supernatural and giving you a biblical foundation for making sense of what you see. Includes a comprehensive Dream Symbols Dictionary with over 1,000 biblical definitions.

Seeing the Voice of God

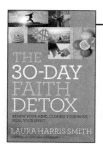

Invisible faith toxins can cause symptoms that affect our entire being—mind, body and spirit. In this one-month detox, expert Laura Harris Smith uncovers thirty faith toxins and promotes biblical healing of the whole person through prayer, Scripture and simple recipes. Refresh and refuel yourself spiritually, mentally and physically with this practical guide.

30-Day Faith Detox

✓Chosen

 Stay up to date on your favorite books and authors with our free e-newsletters. Sign up today at chosenbooks.com.

 facebook.com/chosenbooks

 @Chosen_Books

 @chosen_books

You May Also Like . . .

Accessible, practical and grounded in real life, *The Healthy Living Handbook* is full of simple, everyday ways to live a truly healthy life—body, mind and spirit. These easy-to-implement lifestyle tips will not only bring the peace, rest, energy, connection and clarity you've been longing for, but help you to live better in every area of life.

The Healthy Living Handbook

Leaving no stone unturned, certified nutritional counselor, pastor, and TV host Laura Harris Smith helps you pursue healing and wellness both naturally and supernaturally. She shows how both are necessary to living an abundant life, and she equips you with the tools you need for the journey, including tailored menus, healing prayers and practical tips.

Get Well Soon